"All scripture is given by inspiration of God,
and is profitable for doctrine, for reproof, for correction,
for instruction in righteousness:
that the man of God may be perfect,
thoroughly furnished to do all good works."

—2 Timothy 3:16 & 17

"For whatsoever things were written previously were written for our learning,
that we through patience and comfort of the scriptures might have hope."

—Romans 15:4

ETERNAL PERSPECTIVE:

Connecting the Crimson Dots of His Covenant

DJ JACKSON

Carpenter's Son Publishing

Eternal Perspective: Connecting the Crimson Dots of His Covenant

©2018 by D J Jackson

Published by Carpenter's Son Publishing, Franklin, Tennessee

Published in association with Larry Carpenter of Christian Book Services LLC of Franklin, Tennessee

Illustrated by D J Jackson

Edited by Adept Content Solutions

Cover and Interior Design by Suzanne Lawing

ISBN: 978-1-946889-41-6

Printed in the United States of America

WITH MY DEEPEST LOVE AND GRATITUDE TO:

God who gets all the glory for the inspiration.
His depth of love for us is almost hard to believe.
His gift of redemption through His Word
and Holy Spirit is so amazing.

W - My beloved husband and gift from God.

David & Jean - My beloved parents, whose
prayers, love, encouragement and generosity have
made the first print run possible.

Many dear friends and family members who have
blessed me over the years, through their encouragement,
prayers, investment in the artwork, and editing skills.

CONTENTS

Welcome to

Eternal Perspective:

Connecting the Crimson Dots of His Covenant

by DJ Jackson ©2017

Visiting Israel, it became visually apparent that there are several perspectives on religion represented. Each one stands firm in their beliefs, but not all of them worship the same God. Looked at through the lens of history and documented facts from ancient manuscripts, along with archeological evidence and fulfilled prophecies, this exhibit challenges you to consider the deep questions relating to the land of Israel.

All images are original oil paintings on canvas created from photographs I took on a recent trip to Israel. It was a journey that helped me to connect the covenant dots in the trail left by our Creator and Master Artist. See if you can locate the physical crimson dot in each painting as well as comprehend the ones that connect this entire story. This narrative (book) accompanies a traveling art exhibit that displays the original paintings.

I pray that as you view these paintings and read the words accompanying them that the very Spirit of God will move you to seek out the way, the truth, and the life. With love and His peace.

DO WE AS A CIVILIZATION KNOW OUR HERITAGE?

Every story has a beginning and an end: the creator writes these bookends and everything in between. The perspective that this exhibit will highlight is the one written by our Master Creator, King of the Universe. This story is an eternal one . . . so let's start with eternity in mind, beginning with the end of the story. We will consider what many still believe to be prophecy yet to be fulfilled. This story is documented through scribes in ancient manuscripts and written as paraphrased sound bites.

We will begin our journey with an image painted from a photograph of one of the ruins in Megiddo. This painting represents the *"restitution of all things"* (Acts 3:20–21) that is to occur at the end of the age. It is when God will *"restore the years that the locust have eaten . . ."* and is titled "Reaping In Due Season."

In a vision that the apostle John was shown documented in the book of Revelation 21:1—22:21 written circa 95 AD, the end to our story is described as *"the holy city, new Jerusalem coming down from God out of heaven …the tabernacle of God with men, where God himself will dwell among us . . . And God will wipe away all tears from their eyes; and there shall be no more death, neither sorrow, nor crying, neither shall there be any more pain: for the former things are passed away. And he that sat upon the throne said, 'Behold, I make all things new.' And he said to me, 'Write, for these words are TRUE and faithful.' And he said to me, 'It is done. I am Alpha and Omega, the beginning and the end. I will give to him that is thirsty of the fountain of the water of LIFE freely.'"*

• *"'He that OVERCOMES shall inherit all things; and I will be his God, and he shall be my son.' . . . And he showed me a pure river of water of life, clear as crystal, proceeding out of the throne of God and of the Lamb. In the midst of the street of it, and on the other side of the river, there was the tree of life, which bare twelve manner of fruits, and yielded her fruit every month: and the leaves of the tree were for the healing of the nations. And there shall be no more curse: but the throne of God and the Lamb shall be in it; and his servants shall serve him, and they shall see his face, and his name shall be on their foreheads. These sayings are faithful and TRUE: and the Lord God of the holy prophets sent his angel to show to his servants the things which must shortly be done. 'Behold, I come quickly: blessed is he that keeps the sayings of the prophecy of this book . . . And if any man shall take away from the words of the book of this prophecy, God shall take away his part out of the book of life, and out of the holy city, and from the things which are written in this book.'"* The entire book of Revelation is included at the end of this exhibit.

The prophet Joel was given the words in Joel 2:25–32: *"And I will restore to you the years that the locust have eaten . . . And you shall know that I am in the midst of Israel, and that I am the LORD your God, and none else: and my people shall never be ashamed."*

©2017 Reaping In Due Season—Eternal Perspective: Connecting the Crimson Dots of His Covenant

HAVE YOU EVER EXPERIENCED A WILDERNESS SEASON?

Now that we see a glimpse of eternity and what is yet to come, let's start from the beginning. *"In the beginning God created the heaven and the earth. And the earth was without form, and void; and darkness was upon the face of the deep. And the SPIRIT of God moved upon the face of the waters."* All that He created is well documented in Genesis 1:1–3:24.

"And God said, let us make man in our own image, after our likeness . . . And the LORD God formed man of the dust of the ground, and breathed into his nostrils the breath of life; and man became a living SOUL." Adam, the first man, was created in the image of God containing the attributes of a SPIRIT and a SOUL, which are documented as being eternal, and a physical body (flesh), which now has an expiration date on earth. Documented in the book of John, it is recorded that *"In the beginning was the Word, and the Word was with God, and the Word was God. The same was in the beginning with God. All things were made by him; and without him was not any thing made that was made. In him was LIFE; and the LIFE was the light of men . . . and the Word was made flesh and dwelt among us, (and we beheld his glory, the glory as of the only begotten of the Father) full of grace and TRUTH."* In 1 John 5:7 it is recorded, *"For there are three that bear record in heaven, the Father, the Word and the Holy Spirit: and these three are one."*

Recorded back in Genesis, God (Creator) gave Adam a choice to follow His ways and have everlasting life enjoying the physical presence of God. Our Creator's ways were set up to enjoy a perfect, peaceful environment, where Adam lacked nothing. His work was joyful, and he had no knowledge of evil. Adam and the wife God created for him, Eve, chose to eat from the one tree they were commanded not to of all creation given to them: of the tree of the knowledge of good and evil. From the very beginning, our Creator gave us the ability to choose Him and His ways. Instead of following God's instructions, Eve listened to the *"serpent which was more subtle than any beast of the field which the LORD God had made . . . And the LORD GOD said, 'Behold, the man has become as one of us, to know good and evil, and now if he also takes of the tree of life, and eats from it, he will live forever. Therefore the LORD God sent him out of the garden of Eden, to till the ground from where he was taken."* God's intention for man was that he would not know or experience evil, but their choice opened their eyes to the existence of evil. The consequence of their decision was that they immediately experienced a spiritual death and could no longer be in the physical presence of God. In God's mercy, to keep them from living eternally in this state, they and all offspring after this choice would experience a physical death. To cover their offense, the first animal was sacrificed.

• After several generations, it is recorded, *"And God saw that the wickedness of man was great in the earth, and that every imagination of the thoughts of his heart was only evil continually . . . and He was grieved in his heart . . . But Noah found grace in the eyes of the LORD . . . The earth also was corrupt before God, and the earth was filled with violence . . . And God said to Noah, 'The end of all flesh has come before me; for the earth is filled with violence through them, and behold, I will destroy them with the earth . . . But with you I will establish my covenant, and you will come into the ark, your sons, and your wife, and your sons' wives with you. And every living thing of all flesh, two of every sort will you bring into the ark, to keep them alive with you, they shall be male and female...And they went into the ark with Noah, two and two of all flesh, wherein is the breath if life."* So He destroyed all living creation on the earth with a flood, except Noah and his family, and male and female pairs of each animal to repopulate the earth as written in Genesis 6:1–11:32.

• Several generations later, Abram, a descendant of Noah's son Shem, was one of a small amount of people who tried to follow God's ways. Abram (God later changed his name to Abraham) and his wife Sarai (God later changed hers to Sarah) went through a number of tests before God made His covenant with Abraham. *"Now the LORD had said to Abram, 'Get out of your country, and from your kindred, and from your father's house, to a land I will show you; and I will make of you a great nation, and I will bless you, and make your name great, and you shall be a blessing. And I will bless them that bless you, and curse him that curse you, and in you shall all families of the earth be blessed.'"* See Genesis 12:1–25:18 for the backstory.

• It is written in Genesis 15:18–22:18, *"In the same day the LORD made a covenant with Abram, saying 'Unto your seed I have given this land, from the river of Egypt into the great river Euphrates . . . And God said, Sarah your wife shall bear you a son indeed; and you shall call his name Isaac: and I will establish my covenant with him for an everlasting covenant, and with his seed after him . . . And as for Ishmael, I have heard you, behold, I have blessed him, and will make him fruitful, and will multiply him exceedingly. He will have twelve princes, and I will make him a great nation.'"* Several generations later the descendants of Abraham, Isaac and Jacob (God later changed his name to Israel) were in bondage in Egypt.

• *"And it came to pass in the process of time, that the king of Egypt died: and the children of Israel sighed because of their bondage, and they cried, and their cry came up to God because of their bondage. And God heard their groaning, and God remembered his covenant with Abraham, with Isaac, and with Jacob,"* as recorded in Exodus 2:23–24.

• A man named Moses was called to bring the Israelites out of the bondage in Egypt and take them to their Promised Land. As recorded in Exodus 3:13–15, *"And Moses said to God, 'Behold, when I come to the children of Israel, and say to them, 'The God of your fathers has sent me to you;' and they shall say to me, 'What is his name? What shall I say to them?' And God said to Moses, 'I AM THAT I AM:' and he said, 'Thus shall you say to the children of Israel, The LORD God of your fathers, the God of Abraham, Isaac, and Jacob, has sent me to you: this is my name forever, and this is my memorial to all generations.'"* When Moses led the Israelites through the wilderness he called all of them and said *"Hear, Oh Israel, the statutes and judgments which I speak in your ears this day, that you may learn, keep and do them. The LORD our God made a covenant with us in Horeb. He didn't make it with our fathers, but with us, who are all of us here alive this day . . . And God spoke all these words, saying 'I am the LORD your God which brought you out of the land of Egypt, from the house of bondage. You shall have no other gods before me."* His commandments are written out in Deuteronomy 5:1–33 and Exodus 20:1–17.

• Leviticus 20:24 records, "But I have said to you, 'You shall inherit their land, and I will give it to you to possess it, a land that flows with milk and honey. I AM the LORD your God, which has separated you from other people.'" In Leviticus 24:8, it records *"Every sabbath he shall set it in order before the LORD continually, being taken from the children of Israel by an everlasting covenant."* In Exodus 31:16–18 it is also described as a *"perpetual covenant."* In Isaiah 61:8–62:12, God said of the restoration in the millennium *". . . I will make an everlasting covenant with them. And their seed shall be known among the Gentiles."*

• While the Israelites were in the wilderness on their way to their Promised Land, it is documented in Deuteronomy 8:1–20 that God said, *"All the commandments which I command you this day shall you observe to do, that you may live, and multiply, and go in and possess the land which the LORD swore to your fathers. And you shall remember all the ways which the LORD your God led you these forty years in the wilderness, to humble you, and to prove (test) you, to know what was in your heart; whether you would keep his commandments or not. And he humbled you, and allowed you to hunger, and fed you with manna, which neither you nor your fathers knew, so that he might make you know that man does not live by bread alone, but by every word that proceeds out of the mouth of the LORD man does live . . . But you shall remember the LORD your God; for it is he that gives you the power to get wealth, that he may establish his covenant, which he swore to your fathers, as it is this day. And it shall be, that if you do at all forget the LORD your God, and walk after other gods and serve them, and worship them, I testify against you this day that you shall surely perish. As the nations which the LORD destroyed before your face, so shall you perish; because you would not be obedient to the voice of the LORD your God."* Instead of being grateful for their freedom from slavery and bondage, the Israelites complained and did not trust him in their journey to freedom.

In Deuteronomy 28:1–30:20 God laid out the choices given to the Israelites. Their obedience and remembrance of God being the source of abundance would bring them blessings, and disobedience and forgetting this origination of abundance would bring curses. *"I call heaven and earth to record this day against you, that I have set before you LIFE and death, blessing and cursing. Therefore choose LIFE, that both you and your seed may live: that you may love the LORD your God, and that you may obey his voice, and that you will cleave to him. For he is your LIFE, and length of your days: that you may dwell in the land which the LORD swore unto your fathers, to Abraham, to Isaac, and to Jacob, to give them."*

In spite of many generations of disobedience and rebellion against what was laid out for them, our Creator, however, already had a restorative plan to put His creation back on track. This plan is well documented in Genesis, Exodus, Leviticus, Numbers, and Deuteronomy.

This image was created from the wilderness that I saw en route to the Dead Sea. It is painted as a Diptych (two-panel painting) to represent the time of testing in the wilderness that the Covenant people encountered on their way to the Promised Land. It also represents the time when Yeshua (Jesus) was led by the Spirit into the wilderness, before He started His earthly mission. We'll learn in later panels of this exhibit about the Israelites' wilderness experience and Yeshua's (Jesus') experience.

©2017 Moving Mountains With Joy (Diptych)—Eternal Perspective: Connecting the Crimson Dots of His Covenant

HOW WAS THE COVENANT REVEALED?

• *"Hear, Oh Israel: You are to pass over Jordan this day, to go in to possess nations greater and mightier than yourselves, cities great and fenced up to heaven . . ."* recorded in Deuteronomy 9:1. *"The land shall not be sold forever: for the land is mine, for you are strangers and sojourners with me. And in all the land of your possession you shall grant a redemption for the land . . . But the field of the suburbs of their cities may not be sold; for it is their* **perpetual** *possession . . . I am the LORD your God, which brought you forth out of the land of Egypt, to give you the land of Canaan, and to be your God."* This was recorded in Leviticus 25:23–55, and chapter 26 lays out the points of God's covenant and the reverence expected to keep his statutes and commandments. Then His provision, increase, safety, peace, and power would be theirs. *"For I will have respect for you, and make you fruitful, and multiply you, and establish my covenant with you."* It also spells out what would happen if they would choose to despise His statutes, or if their souls would abhor His judgments and not follow all His commandments but break His covenant. The list is quite extensive. He goes on: *"If they will confess their iniquity, and the iniquity of their fathers, with their trespass which they trespassed against me, and that they also have walked contrary to me; and that I have also walked contrary to them, and have brought them into the land of their enemies. If their uncurtailed hearts will be humbled, and they then accept the punishment of their iniquity, then I will remember my covenant with Jacob, and also my covenant with Isaac, and also my covenant with Abraham I will remember; and I will remember the land. And yet for all that, when they are in the land of their enemies, I will not cast them away, neither will I abhor them, to destroy them utterly, and to break my covenant with them: for I am the LORD their God. But I will, for their sakes, remember the covenant of their ancestors, whom I brought forth out of the land of Egypt in the sight of the heathen (Gentile), that I might be their God: I am the LORD."*

Joshua 23:1—24:28 documents how Joshua and Caleb were the ones leading the Israelites to their Promised Land. *"And it came to pass a long time after that the LORD had given rest to Israel from all their enemies . . . And Joshua said to the people, 'Thus says the LORD God of Israel, your fathers dwelt on the other side of the flood in old time, even Terah, the father of Abraham, and the father of Nachor: and they served other gods. And I took your father Abraham from the other side of the flood, and led him throughout all the land of Canaan, and multiplied his seed, and gave him Isaac . . . And I have given you a land for which you did not labor, and cities which you did not build, and you dwelled in them; of the vineyards and olive yards which you did not plant, that you eat. Now therefore fear the LORD, and serve Him in sincerity and in truth: and put away the gods which your fathers served on the other side of the flood, and in Egypt: and you serve the LORD.'*

So Joshua let them depart, every man to his inheritance." Unfortunately, after a span of some hundreds of years, the Israelites fell into idolatry again. They would repeat the cycle of living abundantly blessed, followed by forgetting God was the source of their blessings and worshipping idols, then receiving the course correction in the discipline of God, and then receiving deliverance from God when they repented.

This painting is a scene from the mountaintop ruin of Masada. Several centuries in this journey brought the people of Israel to this place in history and is well documented in Psalms 74, 75, 76, 77, 78, and 79. A temple was built in Jerusalem, and then destroyed. It was rebuilt, but God's chosen ones did not remember the covenant given to Abraham, Isaac, and Jacob. It is recorded in Jeremiah 5:9 *"Shall I not visit for these things? says the LORD. And shall not my soul be avenged on such a nation as this?"* As prophesied later by Yeshua (Jesus), the rebuilt temple was also destroyed in 70 AD, and Masada was the location of the last fighting group of Zealots in 73 AD.

©2017 Hear Mountains of Israel, A Covenant of Peace (Diptych)—Eternal Perspective: Connecting the Crimson Dots of His Covenant

WHAT WAS THE APPOINTED VISITATION?

Even though God had made a covenant with his people, time after time, they did not choose to follow his ways.

• Jeremiah the prophet foretold in 31:31–33 before the fall of Jerusalem circa 587 BC that *"Behold, the days are coming, says the LORD, that I will make a new covenant with the house of Israel, and with the house of Judah: not according to the covenant that I made with their fathers in the day that I took them by the hand to bring them out of the land of Egypt; which my covenant they broke, although I was a husband to them says the LORD. But this shall be the covenant that I will make with the house of Israel. After those days, says the LORD, I will put my law in their inward parts, and write it in their hearts; and will be their God and they shall be my people."*

• We read the fulfillment of this in Luke 1:67–79 when Zacharias, John the Baptist's father, *"was filled with the Holy Spirit, and prophesied, saying, 'Blessed be the Lord God of Israel; for he has visited and redeemed his people, and he has raised up a horn of salvation for us in the house of his servant David; as he spoke by the mouth of his holy prophets which have been since the world began. That we should be saved from our enemies, and from the hand of all that hate us; to perform the mercy promised to our fathers, and to remember his holy covenant; the oath which he swore to our father Abraham, that he would grant to us, that we being delivered out of the land of our enemies might serve him without fear, in holiness and righteousness before him, all the days of our life. And you, child, shall be called the prophet of the Highest; for you shall go before the face of the Lord to prepare his ways; to give knowledge of salvation to his people by the remission of their sins, through the tender mercy of our God. Whereby the dayspring from on high has visited us, to give light to those who sit in darkness and in the shadow of death, and to guide our feet in the way of peace.'"*

• In the scripture of Isaiah 7:14, we read, *"Therefore the Lord himself shall give you a sign; behold, a virgin shall conceive, and bear a son, and shall call his name Immanuel."*

• We see that this prophecy was fulfilled circa 3 BC as recorded in Matthew 1:23–2:2 when the angel of the Lord appeared to Joseph in a dream, saying, *"Behold, a virgin shall be with child, and shall bring forth a son, and they shall call his name Emmanuel (Greek vs Hebrew spelling), which being interpreted is, God with us. Then Joseph being raised from sleep did as the angel of the Lord had instructed him, and took to him his wife: and he knew her not until she had brought forth her firstborn son, and he called his name JESUS (YESHUA)."* Matthew 1:1-17 contains "The Book of the generation of Jesus Christ, the son of David, the son of Abraham.

• James records in 1:17–18, "Every good gift and every perfect gift is from above, and comes down from the Father of lights, with whom is no variableness, neither shadow of turning. Of His own will, He bred us forth with the word of TRUTH, that we should be a kind of first fruits of his creatures."

This painting was created imagining what it might have looked like on the night Yeshua (Jesus) visited the earth. The terrain in Bethlehem overlooking the shepherd's fields was beautiful. Our tour guide informed us that tradition says Yeshua (Jesus) would have been born in a cave and placed in a stone manger.

©2017 An Appointed Visitation—Eternal Perspective: Connecting the Crimson Dots of His Covenant

WHOSE LINEAGE WOULD THE APPOINTED KING COME THROUGH?

It is recorded in Psalm 89:18–37 *"For the LORD is our defence; and the Holy One of Israel is our king. Then you spoke in vision to your holy one, and said, 'I have laid help upon one that is mighty; I have exalted one chosen out of the people. I have found David my servant. With my holy oil I have anointed him. With whom my hand shall be established. My arm also will strengthen him. The enemy shall not exact (impose) upon him; nor the son of wickedness afflict him. But my faithfulness and my mercy shall be with him: and in my name shall his horn (power) be exalted...I will also make him my firstborn, higher than the kings of the earth. My mercy will I keep for him for evermore, and my covenant shall stand fast with him. His seed also will I make to endure for ever, and his throne as the days of heaven. If his children forsake my law, and do not walk in my judgments; if they break my statutes, and do not keep my commandments, then I will visit their transgression with the rod, and their iniquity with stripes (blows or wounds). Nevertheless I will not utterly take my loving kindness from him, nor suffer (set up) my faithfulness to fail. I will not break my covenant, nor alter the thing that is gone out of my lips. Once that I have sworn by my holiness, I will not lie to David. His seed will endure forever, and his throne as the sun before me. It shall be established forever as the moon, and as a faithful witness in heaven. Selah.'"*

It is recorded in 2 Samuel 23:1-5, *"Now these are the last words of David. David the son of Jesse said, and the man who was raised up on high, the anointed of the God of Jacob, and the sweet psalmist of Israel, said, 'The spirit of the LORD spoke by me, and his word was in my tongue. The God of Israel said, the Rock of Israel spoke to me, He that rules over men must be just, ruling in the fear of God. And he shall be as the light of the morning, when the sun rises, even a morning without clouds; as the tender grass springing out of the earth by clear shining after rain. Although my house be not so with God; yet he has made with me an everlasting covenant, ordered in all things, and sure. For this is all my salvation, and all my desire, although he does not make it grow.'"*

This painting was created from an image taken inside the walls of the City of David. The perspective has you looking up to heaven. When you view it, you can remember, "The Heavens declare the glory of God; and the firmament shows His handiwork," (Psalm 19:1).

WHO IS THE LAMB?

The gospel of Mark starts with the words, *"The Beginning of the gospel of Yeshua Ha-Mashiach (Jesus Christ), the Son of God: as it is written in the prophets, 'Behold, I send my messenger before your face, which shall prepare your way before you. The voice of one crying in the wilderness. Prepare the way of the Lord, make his paths straight.' John did baptize in the wilderness, and preach the baptism of repentance for the remission of sins. And all went out to him in the land of Judea, and those of Jerusalem, and were all baptized by him in the river of Jordan, confessing their sins . . . And (John) preached, saying, 'There comes one after me who is mightier than I: the strap of whose sandals I am not worthy to stoop down and unloose.'"*

• The lamb in this scene is symbolic of the description that John the Baptist spoke of when he saw Jesus walking and said, *"Behold the Lamb of God, which takes away the sin of the world . . . And I saw, and bare record that this is the Son of God."* This is written in John 1:29, 34.

• Earlier in history, before the Israelites gained their freedom from Egypt's Pharaoh, God needed to step up the plagues he put on Egypt so that Pharaoh would release the Israelite slaves. It is recorded in Exodus 12:1–14 that they were instructed to take a lamb, without blemish, and give it as the atonement on the night the angel of death would pass over in Egypt. It was instructed that "they shall take of the blood (of the lamb), and strike it on the two side posts and on the upper door post of the houses," so that the angel of death would pass over their house when seeing this, and their firstborn would live. We will later understand that Jesus (the Lamb of God) voluntarily became the final sacrifice, once and for all to cover all of our sins, iniquities, and transgressions. All we have to do is receive the gift of His sacrifice as final reconciliation between us and God.

• This painting is from a location by the Jordan River. This same river is the one that the people of covenant crossed over to enter their Promised Land. It is also the same river that Yeshua (Jesus) was baptized in where the scriptures describe that when he came out of the water, the heavens were opened to him, and he saw the Spirit of God descending in bodily shape like a dove and *"a voice from heaven saying, 'You are my beloved Son, in whom I am well pleased.'"* It is written in Mark 1:11–15, *"And immediately the Spirit drove him into the wilderness. And he was there in the wilderness forty days, tempted of Satan; and was with the wild beasts, and the angels ministered to him . . . Jesus came into Galilee, preaching the gospel of the kingdom of God, and saying, 'The time is fulfilled, and the kingdom of God is at hand: repent and believe the gospel.'"* Great places to find more of the story are found in these scriptures: Mark 1:4–15, John 1:1–37 and 17:1–26, Hebrews 9:11–28, Deuteronomy 18:15–22, Isaiah 53:1–12, Matthew 3:16–17, Luke 3:21–22, Exodus 12:1–14, 1 Peter 1:16–25, and Revelation 5:1—7:17.

©2017 Divine Reconciliation—Eternal Perspective: Connecting the Crimson Dots of His Covenant

WHO DO YOU SAY I AM? FOLLOW ME

This scene is from a view on the Sea of Galilee. Many lessons were taught around this beautiful sea. Matthew 4:13–19 records, *"And leaving Nazareth, he came and dwelt in Capernaum, which is upon the sea coast, in the borders of Zabulon and Nephthalim: that it might be fulfilled which was spoken by Esaias (Isaiah) the prophet, saying, 'the land of Zabulon, and the land of Nephthalim, by the way of the sea, beyond Jordan, Galilee of the Gentiles; the people which sat in darkness saw great light. And to those who sat in the region and shadow of death, light has sprung up.' From that time Jesus began to preach, and to say, 'Repent for the Kingdom of heaven is at hand.' And Jesus, walking by the Sea of Galilee, saw two brothers; Simon called Peter, and Andrew his brother casting a net into the sea . . . and he said to them 'Follow Me, and I will make you fishers of men.'"*

• Several miracles later Jesus asked his disciples, *"But who do you say I am? And Simon Peter answered and said, 'You are the Christ (Messiah in Greek), the Son of the living God.' And Jesus answered and said to him, 'Blessed are you Simon Bar-jona: for flesh and blood has not revealed it to you, but my Father which is in heaven."* This is recorded in Matthew 16:15–17, Mark 8:27–30, and Luke 9:18–22. It is recorded in John 8:58 that Jesus told the Jews, *"Truly, truly, I say to you, before Abraham was, I AM."*

• Through the prophet Isaiah, God spoke as written in Isaiah 48:1—49:26: *"Hear this, Oh house of Jacob, which are called by the name Israel . . . Behold I have refined you, but not with silver; I have chosen you in the furnace of affliction. For my own sake, will I do it: for how should my name be polluted? And I will not give my glory to another. Hearken to me, Oh Jacob and Israel, my called. I AM he, I AM the first, I AM also the last. My hand also has laid the foundation of the earth, and my right hand has spanned the heavens. When I call to them, they stand up together. All you, assemble yourselves, and hear . . . I, even I, have spoken; yes, I have called him, I have brought him, and he shall make his way prosperous. Come near to me, hear this; I have not spoken in secret from the beginning, from the time that it was, there am I. And now the Lord GOD, and his spirit has sent me.' Thus says the LORD, your Redeemer, the Holy One of Israel; 'I AM the LORD your God which teaches you to profit, which leads you by the WAY you should go. Oh that you had hearkened to my commandments! Then your peace would have been as a river, and your righteousness as the waves of the sea. Your seed also would have been as the sand, and the offspring of your bowels like the gravel thereof. His name should not have been cut off nor destroyed before me . . .' Thus says the LORD, 'In an acceptable time have I heard you, and in a day of salvation have I helped you, and I will preserve you, and give you for a covenant of the people, to establish the earth, to cause them to inherit the desolate heritages. So that you may say to the prisoners, 'Go forth, to those who are in darkness, show yourselves.'"*

Later in their time together, Philip asked Jesus to show them the Father. Jesus answered, *"Have I been such a long time with you, and yet have you not known me, Philip? He that has seen me has seen the Father; and how do you say then, show us the Father? Do you not believe that I am in the Father, and the Father is in me? The words that I speak to you, I speak not of myself: but of the Father that dwells in me, he does the works."*

In Matthew 9:35–38 it says, *"And Jesus went about all Galilee, teaching in their synagogues, and preaching the gospel of the kingdom, and healing all manner of sickness and all manner of disease among the people. But when Jesus saw the multitudes, he was filled with compassion for them because they fainted and were scattered abroad, as sheep having no shepherd. Then he said to his disciples, 'The harvest truly is plenteous, but the laborers are few; pray therefore that the Lord of the harvest will send forth laborers into his harvest.'"*

©2017 Follow Me—Eternal Perspective: Connecting the Crimson Dots of His Covenant

WHAT IS DIVINE STRENGTH & POWER?

• The tree on pages 26-27 is composed of eight panels representing the Tree of Life. Each panel tells a story or several relating to the kingdom of God, and His divinity. The paintings are a composite of three different trees photographed around Capernaum with the Sea of Galilee in the background. Psalm 105:4–45 records, *"Seek the LORD, and His strength: seek His face evermore. Remember his marvelous works that he has done; his wonders, and the judgments of his mouth; you seed of Abraham his servant, you children of Jacob his chosen. He is the LORD our God: his judgments are in all the earth. He has remembered his covenant forever, the word which he commanded to a thousand generations, which covenant He made with Abraham, and His oath to Isaac; and confirmed the same to Jacob for a law, and to Israel for an everlasting covenant . . ."* King David is recorded as saying in 2 Samuel 22:33, *"God is my strength and power, and he makes my way perfect."*

In Isaiah 40:28–31 it is written, *"Have you not known? Have you not heard, that the everlasting God, the LORD, the Creator of the ends of the earth, faints not, neither is weary? There is no searching of his understanding. He gives power to the faint; and to those who have no might he increases strength. Even the youths shall faint and be weary, and the young men shall utterly fall; but they that wait upon the LORD shall renew their strength. They shall mount up with wings as eagles; they shall run, and not be weary; and they shall walk, and not faint."*

Yeshua (Jesus) told Simon Peter in Matthew 16:19, *"And I will give to you the keys of the kingdom of heaven: and whatever you will bind on earth, will be bound in heaven: and whatever you loose on earth will be loosed in heaven."*

After Jesus ascended, which we will see in a later panel, the apostle Paul wrote to the Ephesians recorded in 6:10–20: *"Finally, my brothers, be **strong in the Lord**, and in the **power of his might**. Put on the whole armor of God, that you may be able to stand against the wiles (tricks) of the devil. For we wrestle not against flesh and blood, but against principalities, against powers, against the rulers of the darkness of this world, against spiritual wickedness in high places. Wherefore take unto you the whole armor of God, that you may be able to withstand in the evil day, and having done all, to stand. Stand therefore, having your loins (hips) fastened with your belt of TRUTH, and having on the breastplate of righteousness, and put shoes on your feet with the preparation of the gospel of peace. Above all, taking the shield of faith, wherewith you shall be able to quench all the fiery darts of the wicked. And take the helmet of salvation, and the sword of the Spirit, which is the word of God: praying always with all prayer and supplication (requests) in the Spirit, and watching there-*

fore with all perseverance and supplication for all saints. And for me, that utterance may be given to me, that I may boldly open my mouth, to make known the mystery of the gospel, of which I am an ambassador in bonds, that therein I may speak boldly, as I ought to speak."

©2017 Divine Strength & Power—Eternal Perspective: Connecting the Crimson Dots of His Covenant

WHAT IS DIVINE PROVISION?

• As it was spoken to the Israelites in Deuteronomy 8:18–20, they were exhorted to *"remember the LORD your God: for it is he that gives us power to get wealth, that he may establish his covenant which he swore to your fathers, as it is this day. And it will be that if you do at all forget the LORD your God, and walk after other gods, and serve them, and worship them, I testify against you this day that you will surely perish. As the nations which the LORD destroyed before your face, so will you perish; because you would not be obedient to the voice of the LORD your God."*

When Jesus was teaching, it is written in Matthew 6:25–34 that He said, *"Therefore I say to you, take no thought for your life, what you will eat, or what you will drink, nor for what you will wear. Is not the life more than meat, and the body more than raiment (clothing)? Look at the fowls of the air, for they neither sow, nor reap, nor gather into barns, yet your heavenly Father feeds them. Are you not more valuable than they? Which of you by taking thought can add one cubit (measure) to his stature? And why do you care about your clothes? Consider the lilies of the field, how they grow. They do not toil, neither do they spin, and yet I say to you that even Solomon in all his glory was not arrayed like one of these. Wherefore, if God so clothes the grass of the field, which is here today and tomorrow is cast into the oven, shall he not much more clothe you? Oh you of little faith? Therefore take no thought, saying, 'What shall we eat?' or 'What shall we drink?' or 'With what will we be clothed?' For the Gentiles seek after all these things, and your heavenly Father knows that you have need of all of these things. But seek first the kingdom of God, and his righteousness, and all these things shall be added to you. Therefore take no thought for tomorrow, for tomorrow will have its own concerns. Each day is filled with its share of evil."*

• As we will see in a later panel, the greatest provision of all was Yeshua (Jesus) himself, who came to earth to be our mediator as documented in 1 Timothy 2:5–6 *"For there is one God, and one mediator between God and men, the man Yeshua Ha-Mashiach (Christ Jesus); who gave himself a ransom for all, to be testified in due time."* It is written in 1 Peter 1:17–23, *"And if you call on the Father, who without respect of persons judges according to every man's work, pass the time of your sojourning here in fear: forasmuch as you know that you were not redeemed with corruptible things, as silver and gold, from your vain conversation received by tradition from your fathers. But by the precious blood of Christ, as of a lamb without blemish and without spot: who truly was foreordained before the foundation of the world, but was manifest in these last times for you, who by him do believe in God, that raised him up from the dead, and gave him glory. That your faith and hope might be in God."*

It is written in Hebrews 13:8–9, *"Jesus Christ is the same yesterday, and today, and forever. Do not be carried away with divers (clashing) and strange doctrines. For it is a good thing that the heart is established with grace; not with meats which have not profited those who have been occupied therein."* In John 4:34 it records, *"Jesus said to them, 'My meat is to do the will of Him that sent me, and to finish His work.'"*

©2017 Divine Provision—Eternal Perspective: Connecting the Crimson Dots of His Covenant

WHAT IS DIVINE HEALING?

Matthew 8:5–13 records, *"And when Jesus had entered Capernaum, a centurion came to him beseeching (calling) him, and saying, 'Lord, my servant lies at home sick of the palsy, grievously tormented.' And Jesus said to him, 'I will come and heal him.' The centurion answered and said, 'Lord, I am not worthy of you coming under my roof, but only speak the word, and my servant will be healed . . . ' When Jesus heard it, he marveled, and said to those who followed, 'Truly I say to you, I have not found such great faith, no, not in Israel. And I say to you, that many shall come from the east and west, and shall sit down with Abraham, Isaac, and Jacob, in the kingdom of heaven. But the children of the kingdom shall be cast out into outer darkness: there shall be weeping and gnashing of teeth.' And Jesus said to the centurion, Go your way and as you have believed, so it shall be done to you.' And his servant was healed in the same hour."* To clarify the meaning of "children of the kingdom," it is written in Matthew 13:34–43 that *"All these things Jesus spoke to the multitude in parables; and he didn't speak without the parables, that it might be fulfilled what was spoken by the prophet, saying, 'I will open my mouth in parables; I will utter things which have been kept secret from the foundation of the world.' Then Jesus sent the multitude away, and went into the house. His disciples came to him saying, 'Declare to us the parable of the tares of the field.' He answered and said to them, 'He that sows good seed is the Son of man; the field is the world; the good seed are the children of the kingdom; but the tares are the children of the wicked one. The enemy that sowed them is the devil. The harvest is the end of the world; and the reapers are the angels. As therefore the tares are gathered and burned in the fire; so it shall be at the end of this world. The Son of man shall send forth his angels, and they shall gather out of his kingdom all things that offend, and those which do iniquity; and will cast them into a furnace of fire: there shall be wailing and gnashing of teeth. Then shall the righteous shine forth as the sun in the kingdom of their Father. He who has ears to hear, let him hear."*

• We will see in a later panel the fulfillment of the prophesied words in Isaiah 53:5 that the Messiah was *". . . wounded for our transgressions, he was bruised for our iniquities. The chastisement (disciplinary correction) of our peace was upon him; and by his stripes (wounds) we are healed."*

We will also see in a later panel that the finished work of Messiah's sacrifice now enables us to receive healing through His Spirit. It is written in Romans 8:26–28, *"Likewise the Spirit also helps our infirmities. For we do not know what we should pray for as we ought, but the Spirit itself makes intercession for us with groaning which cannot be uttered. And he that searches the hearts knows what the mind of the Spirit is because he makes intercession for the saints according to his purpose. And we know that all things work together for good to those who love God, to those who are called according to his purpose."*

We are living in a day of opportunity. The LORD gave us all a promise documented in 2 Chronicles 7:14: "*If my people, which are called by my name, shall humble themselves, and pray, and seek my face, and turn from their wicked ways; then I will hear from heaven, and will forgive their sin, and will heal their land.*"

©2017 Divine Healing—Eternal Perspective: Connecting the Crimson Dots of His Covenant

WHAT IS DIVINE FAITH?

• In John 13:1, 34 it is written, *"Now before the feast of the passover, when Jesus knew that his hour had come that he should depart out of this world to the Father, having loved his own which were in the world, he loved them to the end . . . 'A new commandment I give to you, that you love one another; as I have loved you, that you also love one another.'"* He went on to say in John 14:1–7 *"'Do not let your hearts be troubled: You believe in God, believe also in me. In my Father's house are many mansions, if it were not so, I would have told you. I go to prepare a place for you. And if I go and prepare a place for you, I will come again, and receive you to myself; that where I am, there you may be also. And where I go you know, and you know the WAY.' Thomas said to him, 'Lord, we do not know where you are going, and how can we know the WAY?' Jesus said to him, 'I AM the WAY, the TRUTH, and the LIFE: no man comes to the Father, but by me. If you had known me, you would have known my Father also: and from this time on you know Him, and have seen Him.'"*

Jesus said to his disciples *"you will be hated of all men for my name's sake: but he that endures to the end will be saved . . . Do not fear them because there is nothing covered, that will not be revealed; and hid, that shall not be known . . . And do not fear them which kill the body, but are not able to kill the soul: but rather fear him which is able to destroy both soul and body in hell. Are not two sparrows sold for more than a farthing (Roman coin)? And not one of them shall fall on the ground without your Father (in heaven knowing). But the very hairs of your head are numbered. Do not fear because you are more valuable than many sparrows. Whoever therefore will confess me before men, him will I also confess before my Father which is in heaven . . . But whoever denies me before men, I will also deny him before my Father which is in heaven."* This is recorded in Matthew 10:22–33 and Luke 12:1–12.

• *"The secret things belong to the LORD our God: but those things which are revealed belong to us and to our children forever, that we may do all the words of this law,"* according to Deuteronomy 29:29.

• It is written later in the book of Hebrews 11:1—12:2: *"Now faith is the substance of things hoped for, the evidence of things not seen . . . Through faith we understand that the worlds were framed by the word of God, so that things which are seen were not made of things which do appear."* Romans 4:20–25 records Abraham trusted God: *". . . He staggered not at the promise of God through unbelief; but was strong in faith, giving glory to God. And being fully persuaded that, what He (God) had promised, he was able also to perform. And therefore it was imputed to him for righteousness. Now it was not written for his sake alone, that it was imputed to him; but also for us, to whom it shall be imputed, if we believe on Him that raised up Jesus our Lord from the dead; who was delivered for our offenses, and was raised again for our justification."* 2 Corinthians 4:17–18 documents, *"For our light affliction, which is but for a moment, works for us a far more exceeding and eternal weight of glory; while we look not at the things which are seen, but at the things which are not seen. For the things which are seen are temporal; but the things which are not seen are eternal."*

©2017 Divine Faith—Eternal Perspective: Connecting the Crimson Dots of His Covenant

WHAT IS DIVINE PRAYER?

Jesus is recorded as saying in John 15:16–17, *"You have not chosen me, but I have chosen you, and ordained you, that you should go and bring forth fruit, and that your fruit should remain: that whatsoever you shall ask of the Father in my name, he may give it to you."*

Jesus said that men ought to always pray, and not to faint: *"And will not God avenge his own elect, which cry out day and night to him, though he bears long with them? I tell you that he will avenge them speedily. Nevertheless when the Son of man comes (returns), shall he find faith on the earth?"*

When Jesus taught his disciples and a multitude of people who gathered, on how to pray, he said, *"And when you pray, do not be as the hypocrites: for they love to pray standing in the synagogues and in the corners of the streets, that they may be seen of men. Truly, I say to you, they have their reward. But you, when you pray, do not use vain repetitions, as the heathen (Gentiles) do: for they think that they will be heard for their excessive words. Therefore, do not be like them, for your Father knows what things you need before you ask him. After this manner therefore pray: Our Father who is in heaven, Hallowed (Holy, Pure) be your name. Your kingdom come, your will be done on earth, as it is in heaven. Give us this day our daily bread. And forgive us our debts, as we forgive our debtors. And lead us not into temptation, but deliver us from evil: for yours is the kingdom, and the power, and the glory, for ever. Amen. For if you forgive men their trespasses, your heavenly Father will also forgive you. But if you do not forgive men their trespasses, neither will your Father forgive your trespasses."* This was written in Matthew 6:5–15. Jesus also said in Luke 6:27–28 *"But I say to you which hear, love your enemies, do good to those who hate you, bless those who curse you, and pray for those who despitefully use you."*

James, one of Jesus' disciples wrote in James 5:13–16, *"Is any among you afflicted? Let him pray. Is any merry? Let him sing psalms. Is any sick among you? Let him call for the elders of the church; and let them pray over him, anointing him with oil in the name of the Lord: and the prayer of faith will save the sick, and the Lord will raise him up. And if he has committed sins, they shall be forgiven. Confess your faults one to another, and pray for one another, that you may be healed. The effectual fervent prayer of a righteous man avails much."*

In Paul's epistle, 1 Thessalonians 5:17–25, it is written, *"Pray without ceasing. In every thing give thanks: for this is the will of God in Christ Jesus concerning you. Do not quench the Spirit. Do not despise prophesying. Prove all things; hold fast to that which is good. Abstain from all appearance of evil, and the very God of peace will sanctify you wholly. And I pray God your whole SPIRIT and SOUL and BODY be preserved blameless unto the coming of our Lord Jesus Christ. Faithful is he that calls you, who will also do it. Brothers, pray for us."*

©2017 Divine Prayer—Eternal Perspective: Connecting the Crimson Dots of His Covenant

WHAT IS DIVINE PROTECTION (PRESERVATION)?

• In John 15:1–16:33 Jesus taught his disciples how to overcome by saying . . . *"If you abide in me, and my words abide in you, you shall ask what you will, and it shall be done unto you. Herein my Father is glorified, that you bear much fruit; so you shall be my disciples. As the Father has loved me, so I have loved you; continue in my love. If you keep my commandments, you will abide in my love; even as I have kept my Father's commandments and abide in His love. These things I have spoken to you, that my joy might remain in you, and that your joy might be full. This is my commandment, 'That you love one another, as I have loved you . . .' If the world hates you, you know that it hated me before it hated you . . . If I had not done among them the works which no other man had done, they would not have sinned. But now they have both seen and hated both me and my Father. But this has come to pass, that the word that is written in their law might be fulfilled. They hated me without a cause. But when the Comforter (Holy Spirit) comes, whom I will send to you from the Father, even the Spirit of TRUTH, which continues (proceeds) from the Father, he will testify of me. And you shall also be a witness, because you have been with me from the beginning. These things I have spoken to you, that you should not be offended. They will put you out of the synagogues. Yes, the time is coming, that whosoever kills you will **think** that he is doing God a service. And these things they will do to you, because they have not known the Father, nor me. But these things I have told you, that when the time shall come, you may remember that I told you of them. And these things I didn't say to you at the beginning, because I was with you . . . Nevertheless I tell you the TRUTH, it is expedient for you that I go away. For if I do not go away, the Comforter will not come to you; but if I depart, I will send him to you . . . Howbeit when he, the Spirit of TRUTH, has come, he will guide you into all TRUTH: for he shall not speak of himself; but whatsoever he hears, he will speak, and he will show you things to come."*

• Our divine protection is also written about in Psalm 121: *"I will lift up my eyes to the hills, from where my help comes. My help comes from the LORD, which made heaven and earth. He will not cause your foot to be moved. He that keeps you will not slumber. Behold, he that keeps Israel will neither slumber nor sleep. The LORD is your keeper; the LORD is your shade on your right hand. The sun shall not smite you by day, nor the moon by night. The LORD shall preserve (protect) you from all evil; he shall preserve your soul. The LORD shall preserve your going out and your coming in from this time forth, and even for evermore."*

"He that dwells in the secret place of the most High shall abide under the shadow of the Almighty. I will say of the LORD, He is my refuge and my fortress: my God; in him I will trust. Surely he will deliver you from the

snare of the fowler, and from the noisome pestilence. He shall cover you with his feathers, and under his wings you shall trust: his TRUTH shall be your shield and buckler (protection surrounding you). You shall not be afraid of the terror by night, nor wounded by the arrow that flies by day, nor for the pestilence that walks in darkness, nor for destruction that wastes at noonday . . ." as recorded in Psalm 91.

©2017 Divine Preservation—Eternal Perspective: Connecting the Crimson Dots of His Covenant

WHAT IS DIVINE MULTIPLICATION?

• It is written in Matthew 14:14–21, *"And Jesus went forth, and saw a great multitude, and was moved with compassion toward them, and he healed their sick. And when it was evening, his disciples came to him, saying, 'This is a desert place, and the time is now past. Send the multitude away, so that they may go into the villages, and buy victuals (meat) for themselves.' But Jesus said to them, 'They need not depart; you give them something to eat.' And they said to him, 'We have only five loaves, and two fish.' He said, 'Bring them over to me.' And he commanded the multitude to sit down on the grass, and took the five loaves, and the two fish, and looking up to heaven, he blessed it, and broke the bread, and gave the loaves to his disciples, and they gave it to the multitude. And they all ate, and were full, and they took up the fragments that remained which were twelve baskets full. And they that had eaten were about five thousand, beside women and children."* He repeated the miracle of multiplication again, as recorded in Matthew 15:33–39.

• It is written in John 6:26–40 *". . . Jesus answered them and said, 'Truly, truly, I say to you, You seek me, not because you saw the miracles, but because you did eat of the loaves, and were filled. Do not labor for the meat that perishes, but for that meat which endures to everlasting LIFE, which the Son of man shall give to you, for God the Father has sealed (marked for security or preservation) Him.' Then they said to him, 'What shall we do that we might do the works of God?' Jesus answered and said to them, 'This is the work of God, that you believe in him who he has sent.' They said therefore to him, 'What sign do you show then, that we may see, and believe you? What work will you do? Our fathers did eat manna in the desert; as it is written, he gave them bread from heaven to eat.'*

• *Then Jesus said to them, 'Truly, truly, I say to you, Moses did not give you bread from heaven; but my Father gives the true bread from heaven. For the bread of God is he which comes down from heaven, and gives LIFE to the world.' Then they said to him, 'Lord, forevermore give us this bread.' And Jesus said to them, 'I AM the bread of LIFE; he that comes to me shall never hunger; and he that believes in me shall never thirst. But I say to you, that you also have seen me, and do not believe. All that the Father gives me shall come to me; and he that comes to me I will not cast out. For I came down from heaven, not to do my own will, but the will of him that sent me. And this is the Father's will which has sent me, that all which he has given to me I should not lose any, but should raise up again at the last day. And this is the will of him that sent me, that every one which sees the Son, and believes on him, may have everlasting life. And I will raise him up at the last day.'"*

Before Jesus' earthly ministry, he was in the wilderness for forty days, and he was tempted by the devil. Jesus had not eaten anything and was hungry. It is recorded in Luke 4:1–14 that *"the devil said to him, 'If you are the Son of God, command this stone and it will be made bread.' And Jesus answered him, saying, 'It is written, That man shall not live by bread alone, but by every word of God.'"*

©2017 Divine Multiplication—Eternal Perspective: Connecting the Crimson Dots of His Covenant

WHAT IS DIVINE SALVATION?

• It is written in Luke 19:1–11 that Jesus said to Zacchaeus, a wealthy chief tax collector, who climbed up a sycamore tree to see him amongst the crowd, *"This day salvation has come to this house, for so much as he also is a son of Abraham. For the Son of man has come to seek and to save that which was lost."* And in a conversation later with his disciples, on the Mount of Olives, Jesus was speaking in a parable about the kingdom of heaven and essentially said that once the *"door was shut,"* it would be too late. Matthew 25:1–13 records his words.

• The prophet Isaiah described the coming Messiah as it is written in Isaiah 53:1–12: *"Who has believed our report, and to whom is the arm of the LORD revealed? For he shall grow up before him as a tender plant, and as a root out of a dry ground. He has no form nor comeliness, and when we shall see him, there is no beauty that we should desire him. He is despised and rejected of men, a man of sorrows, and acquainted with grief. And we hid as it were our faces from him; he was despised, and we esteemed him not. Surely he has borne our griefs, and carried our sorrows, yet we did esteem him stricken, smitten of God, and afflicted. But he was wounded for our transgressions, he was bruised for our iniquities, the chastisement of our peace was upon him, and with his stripes (wounds) we are healed. All we like sheep have gone astray; we have turned every one to his own way; and the LORD has laid on him the iniquity of us all. He was oppressed, and he was afflicted, yet he did not open his mouth. He is brought as a lamb to the slaughter, and as a sheep before the shearers is dumb, he also did not open up his mouth. He was taken from prison and from judgement, and who shall declare his generation? For he was cut off from the land of the living, for the transgression of my people he was stricken. And he made his grave with the wicked, and with the rich in his death, because he had done no violence, neither was there any deceit in his mouth. Yet it pleased the LORD to bruise him. He has put him to grief. When you will make his soul an offering for sin, he shall see his seed, he shall prolong his days, and the pleasure of the LORD shall prosper in this land. He shall see the travail (grievance) of his soul, and shall be satisfied. By his knowledge my righteous servant will justify (cleanse) many, for he shall bear their iniquities. Therefore I will divide him a portion with the great, and he shall divide the spoil with the strong, because he has poured out his soul unto death. And he was numbered with the transgressors, and he bore the sin of many, and made intercession for the transgressors."*

• In a conversation with a woman at Jacob's well documented in John 4:7-26, Jesus asked her to give him a drink. Her response back to him caused Jesus to say, *"If you knew the gift of God, and who it is that asked you, 'Give me a drink,' you would have asked him for a drink, and he would have given you living water...*

whosoever drinks of the water that I will give him shall never thirst. But the water that I shall give him will be in him a well of water springing up into everlasting life." He additionally said to her, "Woman, believe me, the hour is coming when you will neither in this mountain, nor at Jerusalem, worship the Father. You worship what you do not know. We know what we worship, for salvation is of the Jews. But the hour is coming, and now is, when the true worshippers shall worship the Father in spirit and in truth; for the Father seeks such to worship him. God is a Spirit: and they that worship him must worship him in spirit and in truth.' The woman said to him, 'I know that when Messiah comes, which is called Christ: when he comes, he will tell us all things.' Jesus said to her, 'I that speak to you am he.'"

©2017 Divine Salvation—Eternal Perspective: Connecting the Crimson Dots of His Covenant

WHAT IS DIVINE BEAUTY?

This scene is painted from a photograph taken from the Mount of Beatitudes, where Jesus taught his disciples as written in Matthew 5:1–19: *"And seeing the multitudes, he went up into a mountain, and when he was set, his disciples came to him. And he opened his mouth and taught them, saying, 'Blessed are the poor in spirit, for theirs is the kingdom of heaven. Blessed are they that mourn, for they shall be comforted. Blessed are the meek, for they shall inherit the earth. Blessed are they which hunger and thirst after righteousness, for they shall be filled. Blessed are the merciful, for they shall obtain mercy. Blessed are the pure in heart, for they shall see God. Blessed are the peacemakers, for they shall be called children of God. Blessed are they which are persecuted for righteousness' sake, for theirs is the kingdom of heaven. Blessed are you, when men will revile (taunt) you, and persecute you, and say all manner of evil against you falsely, for my sake. Rejoice, and be exceeding glad, for great is your reward in heaven, for they also persecuted the prophets which were before you. You are the salt of the earth, but if the salt has lost his savour, wherewith shall it be salted? It is then good for nothing, but to be cast out, and to be trodden underfoot of men. You are the light of the world. A city that is set on a hill cannot be hidden. Neither do men light a candle, and hide it, but put it on a candlestick; and it gives light to all who are in the house. Let your light so shine before men, that they may see your good works, and glorify your Father which is in heaven."*

• *"Don't think that I came to destroy the law, or the prophets, I did not come to destroy, but to FULFILL. For I say to you, Until heaven and earth pass, not one jot or tittle will be removed from the law, until all is fulfilled. Whoever therefore breaks one of the least of these commandments, and shall teach men to do so also, he shall be called the least in the kingdom of heaven. But whoever does and teaches them, the same will be called great in the kingdom of heaven . . ."* Jesus had much more to say to his followers in Matthew 5:20–48.

It is prophesied in the book of Isaiah 52:1–7, *"Awake, awake, put on your strength, Zion, put on your beautiful garments, Jerusalem, the holy city, for henceforth no one who is not stripped of defilement will enter. Shake yourself from the dust; arise and sit down Jerusalem, loose yourself from the bands of your neck, captive daughter of Zion. For thus says the LORD, you have sold yourselves for nought; and you shall be redeemed without money . . .' For thus says the LORD God, 'My people went down before this time into Egypt to sojourn there and the Assyrian oppressed them without cause. Now therefore . . . My name continually everyday is blasphemed. Therefore my people shall know my name, they shall know that I AM he that speaks, behold, it is I. How beautiful on the mountains are the feet of him that brings good tidings, that publishes peace, that brings good tidings of goodness, that publishes salvation; that says to Zion, 'Your God reigns!'"*

This painting, along with several others, has a dim appearance representing that we are seeing things as if through a glass dimly.

©2017 Divine Beauty—Eternal Perspective: Connecting the Crimson Dots of His Covenant

WHAT DOES TRUE PEACE LOOK AND FEEL LIKE?

• This painting is a scene overlooking the Sea of Galilee. It also represents many miracles and stories written in the scriptures found in Matthew 8:23–27, Mark 4:36–41, Luke 8:23–25 and John 14:6–31. It was prophesied in Isaiah 9:6, *"For unto us a child is born, unto us a son is given: and the government shall be upon his shoulder: and his name shall be called Wonderful, Counselor, The mighty God, The everlasting Father, The Prince of PEACE."*

• In Isaiah 54:1–17, Israel's future redemption and the Gentiles' future inheritance is prophesied. *"For your maker is your husband; the LORD of hosts is his name; and your Redeemer the Holy One of Israel. The God of the whole earth shall he be called. For the LORD has called you as a woman forsaken and grieved in spirit, and as a young wife, when you were refused, says your God. For a small moment I have forsaken you; but with great mercies I will gather you. In a little wrath I hid my face from you for a moment; but with everlasting kindness I will have mercy on you, says the LORD your redeemer. For this is as the waters of Noah to me. For as I have sworn that the waters of Noah should no more go over the earth; so I have sworn that I would not be angry with you nor rebuke you. For the mountains will depart, and the hills be removed; but my kindness will not depart from you, neither shall the covenant of my peace be removed, says the LORD that has mercy on you."*

When Jesus walked the earth, this was the area where he and his disciples were traveling by ship on the Sea of Galilee when a great storm arose. Fearful that they would all perish, the disciples woke Jesus who rebuked the wind, and said to the sea *"'Peace, be still.' And the wind ceased, and there was a great calm . . . And (the disciples) feared exceedingly, and said to one another, 'What manner of man is this, that even the wind and the sea obey him?'"* This is recorded in Mark 4:37–39.

• Later it is recorded in John 16:33 that as Jesus was describing what was to become of him, He said, *"These things I have spoken to you, that in me you might have peace. In the world you will have tribulation: but be of good cheer, I have overcome the world."*

• Jesus continues later in this conversation with the disciples and answers a question posed by Judas (not Iscariot): *"If a man loves me, he will keep my words. And my Father will love him, and we will come to him, and make our abode (residence) with him . . . But the Comforter, which is the Holy Spirit, whom the Father will send in my name, he shall teach you all things, and bring all things to remembrance, whatsoever I have said to you. Peace I leave you, my peace I give unto you: not as the world gives, that I give to you. Do not let your heart be troubled, neither let it be afraid."* This is recorded in John 14:1–31.

• It is written in John 8:30–32, *"As he (Jesus) spoke these words, many believed in him. Then he said to those Jews which believed in him, 'If you continue in my word, then you are my disciples indeed; and you will know the TRUTH, and the TRUTH will make you free."*

©2017 Peace Be Still—Eternal Perspective: Connecting the Crimson Dots of His Covenant

WHAT WAS THE GREATEST MISSED APPOINTED VISITATION?

• Before Jesus walked the earth, the prophecy was written in Zechariah 9:9–17 that *". . . Your King is coming to you. He is just, and having salvation; lowly and riding upon . . . the foal of a donkey . . . He shall speak peace to the Gentiles, and his dominion will be from sea to sea, and from the river even to the ends of the earth . . . by the blood of his covenant he will release the prisoners . . ."*

• Before Jesus' sacrifice, he was being celebrated as he was riding on a donkey descending from the Mount of Olives to Jerusalem. *"The whole multitude of the disciples began to rejoice and praise God with a loud voice for all the mighty works that they had seen, saying, 'Blessed be the King that comes in the name of the Lord: peace in heaven, and glory in the highest.' And some of the Pharisees from among the multitude said to him, 'Master, rebuke your disciples.' And he answered and said to them 'I tell you that if these should hold their peace, the stones would immediately cry out.' And when he had come near,* **he beheld the city, and wept over it, saying, 'If you had known, even you, at least in this day, the things which belong to your peace! But now they are hid from your eyes.** *For the days will come upon you, that your enemies will cast a trench around you, and encompass you, and keep you in on every side, and will lay you even with the ground, and your children within you, and they will not leave one stone upon another;* **because you didn't know the time of your VISITATION.'"** This prophecy that Jesus foretold of in Luke 19:37–44, came to pass in 70 AD, when the city of Jerusalem was destroyed.

• Hebrews 1:1–14 records, *"God, who in a great span of time and in many ways spoke in times past to the fathers by the prophets. And has in these last days spoken to us by His Son, whom he has appointed heir of all things. By whom he also made the worlds, who being the brightness of his glory, and the express image of his person, and upholding all things by the word of His power. When he had by himself purged our sins, sat down on the right hand of the Majesty on high. Being made so much better than the angels, as he has by* **inheritance** *obtained a more excellent name than they . . . But to the Son he said, 'Your throne, Oh God, is for ever and ever: a scepter of righteousness is the scepter of your kingdom. You have loved righteousness, and hated iniquity; therefore God, even your God, has anointed you with the oil of gladness above your associates. And, you, Lord, in the beginning have laid the foundation of the earth; and the heavens are the works of your hands. They will perish; but you will remain; and they shall become worn out as a garment does; and as a vesture (covering) you shall fold them up, and they will be changed. But you are the same, and your years will not fail. But to which of the angels did He say at any time, 'Sit on my right hand, until I make your enemies your* *footstool?' Are they not all ministering spirits, sent forth to minister for them who will be heirs of salvation?"*

This image was painted from two different photographs taken. It imagines what it might have looked like over two thousand years ago as Jesus was riding down from the Mount of Olives. Can you picture His view overlooking the city of Jerusalem?

©2017 A Missed Appointment—Eternal Perspective: Connecting the Crimson Dots of His Covenant

WHAT DOES SACRIFICIAL LOVE LOOK LIKE?

• Why was Jesus' (Yeshua's) sacrifice necessary? The explanation of His act is recorded in 1 John 3:1–24. *"Behold, what manner of love the Father has bestowed on us, that we should be called the sons of God . . . and you know that he was manifested to take away our sins, and in him is no sin . . . For this purpose the Son of God, was manifested, that he might destroy the works of the devil."* John 10:7–42 records *"Then Jesus said to them again, 'Truly, truly, I say to you, I am the door of the sheep. All that ever came before me are thieves and robbers: but the sheep did not hear them. I AM the door: if any man enters in by me, he shall be saved, and shall go in and out, and find pasture. The thief comes only to steal, kill, and to destroy. I have come that they might have LIFE, and that they might have it more abundantly. I AM the good shepherd: the good shepherd gives his life for the sheep . . . I AM the good shepherd, and know my sheep, and am known by them. As the Father knows me, even so I know the Father: and I lay down my life for the sheep. And I have other sheep, which are not of this fold. I must also bring them, and they will hear my voice; and there will be one fold, and one shepherd. Therefore, my Father does love me, because I lay down my life, that I might take it again. No man takes it from me, but I lay it down of myself, I have power to lay it down, and I have power to take it again. This commandment I received of my Father . . . I told you, and you did not believe. The works that I do in my Father's name, they bear witness of me. But you do not believe, because you are not of my sheep. As I said to you, my sheep hear my voice, and I know them, and they follow me, and I give to them eternal LIFE, and they shall never perish, neither shall any man pluck them out of my hand. My Father, which gave them to me, is greater than all; and no man is able to pluck them out of my Father's hand. I and my Father are one . . . If I do not do the works of my Father, then do not believe me. But if I do, though you do not believe me, believe the works, that you may know, and believe that the Father is in me, and I in him."*

• When Jesus walked the earth, he was "God with us." Even though he performed supernatural healing, multiplication of food, and acts of great love, compassion, and mercy, the priests and scribes did not recognize his deity. Hebrews 7:22–8:13 documents that Jesus was sent to become a surety of a better covenant. In Hebrews 9:11-26 it is written, *"But Christ (Messiah in the Greek language) who came as high priest of good things to come, by a greater and more perfect tabernacle, not made with hands . . . neither by the blood of goats and calves, but by his own blood he entered once into the holy place, having obtained eternal redemption for us . . . How much more shall the blood of Christ, who through the eternal Spirit offered himself without spot to God, purge your conscience from dead works to serve the living God? And for this cause he is the mediator of the new testament (covenant), that by means of death, for the redemption of the transgressions that were under the first testament, they who are called might receive the promise of eternal inheritance. For where a testament is, there must also of necessity be the death of the testator. For a testament is of force after men are dead: otherwise it is of no strength at all while the testator lives. Whereas neither the first testament was dedicated without blood."*

• *"For when Moses had spoken every precept to all the people according to the law, he took the blood of calves and of goats, with water, and scarlet wool, and hyssop, and sprinkled the book, and all the people, saying, 'This is the blood of the testament (covenant) which God has enjoined to you. Moreover he sprinkled with blood the tabernacle, and all the vessels of the ministry. And almost all things are by the law purged with blood; and without the shedding of blood there is no remission. It was therefore necessary that the patterns of things in heaven should be purified with these; but the heavenly things themselves with better sacrifices than these. For Christ has not entered into the holy places made with hands, which are the figures of the true; but into heaven itself, now to appear in the presence of God for us. Nor still that he should offer himself often, as the high priest entered into the holy place every year with blood of others; for then must he often have suffered since the foundation of the world, but now once in the end of the world he has appeared to put away sin by the sacrifice of himself."*

• It is written in John 14:6–21 that *"Jesus said to him, I AM the WAY, the TRUTH, and the LIFE: no man can come to the Father, but by me . . . Even the Spirit of TRUTH; whom the world cannot receive, because it does not see him. But you know him, for he dwells with you, and shall be with you. I will not leave you comfortless: I will come to you. Yet in a little while, and the world will see me no more. But you will see me, because I live, you will also live. At that day you will know that I AM in my Father, and you in me, and I in you. He that has my commandments, and keeps them, it is he that loves me. And he that loves me shall be loved of my Father, and I will love him, and will manifest myself to him."*

• Before Jesus went to the Garden of Gethsemane with his disciples to pray, he lifted his eyes up to heaven, and said, *"Father, the hour has come; glorify your Son, that your Son also may glorify you. As you have given him power over all flesh, that he should give eternal LIFE to as many as you have given him. And this is LIFE eternal, that they might know you the only true God, and Yeshua Ha-Mashiach (Jesus Christ), whom you have sent. I have glorified you on the earth. I have finished the work which you have given me to do. And now, Father, glorify me with the glory I had with you before the world was. I have manifested your name unto the men which you gave me out of the world. They were yours, and you gave them to me, and they have kept your word."* This was recorded in John 17:1–6.

Under the Old Testament given to Moses, the high priest would offer the blood of calves and goats as a sacrifice for the remission of sins committed. In Leviticus 17:11 it is written, *"For the life of the flesh is* in the blood, and I have given it to you on the altar to make an atonement for your souls: for it is the blood that makes an atonement for the soul." So instead of this ritual continuing, Yeshua (Jesus) came as our High Priest under the new covenant (testament), "but now suffering once in the end of the world he appeared to put away sin by the sacrifice of himself." Jesus became our final sacrifice on Passover as recorded in Hebrews 9:26. Later in the story, the apostle Paul wrote in his epistle to Timothy in 1 Timothy 2:1–6 "I exhort therefore, that first of all, supplications, prayers, intercessions, and giving of thanks, be made for all men; for kings, and for all that are in authority; that we may lead a quiet and peaceable life in all godliness and honesty. For this is good and acceptable in the sight of God our Savior, who would have all men to be saved, and to come to knowledge of the TRUTH. For there is one God, and one mediator between God and men, the man Christ Jesus; who gave himself a ransom for all, to be testified in due time."

• Hebrews 10:1–22 further records, "For the law having a shadow of good things to come, and not the very image of the things, can never with those sacrifices which they offered year after year continually make the worshippers perfect. For then would they not have ceased to be offered? Because that the worshippers once purged should have had no more conscience of sins. But in those sacrifices there is a remembrance again made of sins every year. For it is not possible that the blood of bulls and of goats could take away sins. Therefore when he came into the world, he said . . . 'Sacrifice and offering and burnt offerings and offering for sin you would not, neither had pleasure therein, which are offered by the law.' Then he said, 'Here, I come to do your will, Oh God.' He takes away the first, that he may establish the second. By which we are sanctified through the offering of the body of Jesus Christ once for all. And every priest stands daily ministering and offering often times the same sacrifices, which can never take away sins. But this man, after he had offered one sacrifice for sins for ever, sat down on the right hand of God; from henceforth expecting until his enemies are made a footstool. For by one offering he has perfected for ever those that are sanctified. Whereof the Holy Spirit also is a witness to us: for after that he had said before, 'This is the covenant that I will make with them after those days says the Lord, I will put my laws into their hearts, and in their minds will I write them; and their sins and iniquities I will remember no more."

This painting is a scene from a location in the Garden of Gethsemane. These ancient olive trees have stood witness to many seasons in Israel's history. The cross in the pathway represents our Father's ultimate sacrifice for us. The crimson rose represents the sweat of blood that Messiah experienced before "Saying, Father, if you are willing, remove this cup from me: nevertheless not my will, but yours be done." It also represents the blood that Messiah (Christ) shed for our purification and restoration on the cross as recorded in Luke 22:42–44 and Matthew 26:42.

©2017 Covenant Keeper, A Sacrifice of Love—Eternal Perspective: Connecting the Crimson Dots of His Covenant

WHAT IS THE GREAT CELEBRATION?

• When Jesus rose from the dead as he prophesied would happen, the scriptures tell us that the "Lamb was worthy to open the seven seals that sealed the back of a book." Before Jesus came, no one was found worthy on the earth to open the seals until his sacrifice. A vision was given to the apostle John documented in Revelation 5:1–6: *"And I saw in the right hand of him that sat on the throne a book written within and on the backside, sealed with seven seals. And I saw a strong angel proclaiming with a loud voice, 'Who is worthy to open the book, and to loose the seals thereof?' And no man in heaven, nor in earth, neither under the earth, was able to open the book, neither look thereon. And one of the elders said to me, 'Do not weep, behold the Lion of the tribe of Judah, the Root of David, has prevailed to open the book and to loose the seven seals thereof.' And I beheld, and saw in the midst of the throne and of the four beasts, and in the midst of the elders, stood a Lamb as it had been slain, having seven horns and seven eyes, which are the seven Spirits of God sent forth into all the earth."*

• Acts 2:21–47 records, *"And it shall come to pass, that whoever calls on the name of the Lord shall be saved. You men of Israel, hear these words; Yeshua (Jesus) of Nazareth, a man approved by God among you by miracles and wonders and signs, which God did by him in the midst of you, as you yourselves also know. He was delivered by the determinate counsel and foreknowledge of God, and taken by wicked hands that crucified and killed him. God raised up, having loosed the pains of death, because it was not possible for him to be held by it. For David spoke concerning him, 'I foresaw the Lord always before my face, for he is on my right hand, that I should not be moved: therefore my heart rejoiced, and words were joyful, moreover also my flesh shall rest in hope . . .'"*

• Acts 4:10–12 records, *"Let it be known to you all, and to the people of Israel, that by the name of Yeshua Ha-Mashiach (Jesus Christ) of Nazareth, whom you crucified, whom God raised from the dead, even by him does this man stand here before you whole. This is the stone which the builder's did not set, which has become the head of the corner. Neither is there salvation in any other: for there is no other name under heaven given among men, whereby we must be saved."*

• *"Forasmuch then as the children are partakers of flesh and blood, he also himself likewise took part of the same, that through death he might destroy him that had the power of death, that is, the devil. And delivered them who through the fear of death were all their lifetime subject to bondage. For surely he did not take on the nature of angels; but he took on him the seed of Abraham. Wherefore in all things it behooved him to be made like his brothers, that he might be a merciful and faithful high priest in things pertaining to God, to make rec-*

onciliation for the sins of the people. For in that he himself has suffered being tempted, he is able to help those who are tempted." This is recorded in Hebrews 2:14–18.

This painting was created after visiting the site traditionally known as the Garden Tomb in Jerusalem, Israel. Imagine what it might have looked like over 2,000 years ago, after Yeshua (Jesus) had risen from the dead, as prophesied in the scriptures. For additional backstory on this event see Luke 24:1–53, 1 Timothy 2:5–6, John 16:1—17:26, 1 Thessalonians 5:9–11, Acts 13:29–39, and 2 Peter 1:17–21.

©2017 Confidence In Him—Eternal Perspective: Connecting the Crimson Dots of His Covenant

WHO ASCENDED?

After Jesus rose from the dead as prophesied, he appeared before the eleven in Jerusalem, ate broiled fish and honey, and said to them, *"These are the words which I spoke to you, while I was still with you, that all things must be fulfilled, which were written in the law of Moses, and in the prophets, and in the psalms, concerning me . . . Thus it is written, 'And it behooved Christ to suffer, and rise from the dead the third day: and that repentance and remission of sins should be preached in his name among all nations beginning at Jerusalem. And you are witnesses of these things, and I send the promise of my Father upon you, but stay in Jerusalem until you are endued with power from on high.'"* This account is recorded in Matthew 28:16–20, Mark 16:14–20, and Luke 24:42–53: *"He lifted up his hands while blessing them and was carried up into heaven in a cloud out of their sight."* Acts 1:1–11 also speaks about Jesus' ascension, *"And when he (Jesus) had spoken these words, while they watched, he was taken up; and a cloud received him out of their sight. And while they looked steadfastly toward heaven as he went up, two men stood by in white apparel, and also said '. . . This same Jesus which is taken up from you into heaven, will also come in the same way you saw him go into heaven.'"*

• Zechariah 12:1–14:21 foretold, *". . . Behold the day of the LORD is coming . . . And his feet shall stand in that day on the Mount of Olives, which is before Jerusalem on the east, and the Mount of Olives will cleave in the midst thereof toward the east and the west, and there will be a very great valley; and half of the mountain will move toward the north, and half of it toward the south . . . and the LORD my God will come, and all the saints with him . . . And the LORD will be king over all the earth: in that day there will be one LORD, and his name one."*

• Acts 3:18–26 records, *"But those things, which God before had shown by the mouth of all his prophets, that Messiah (Christ) should suffer, he has so fulfilled. Repent therefore, and be converted, that your sins may be blotted out, when the times of refreshing will come in the presence of the Lord. And he shall send Yeshua Ha-Mashiach (Jesus Christ), which before was preached to you, whom the heaven must receive until the times of restitution of all things, which God has spoken by the mouth of all his holy prophets since the world began. For Moses truly said to the fathers, 'The Lord your God shall raise up a prophet to you of your brothers, like me. Whatever he shall say to you, you need to hear. And it shall come to pass that every soul, which will not hear that prophet, shall be destroyed among the people.' Yes, and all the prophets from Samuel, and those that follow after, as many have spoken, have likewise foretold of these days. You are the children of the prophets, and of the covenant which God made with our fathers, saying to Abraham, 'and in your seed shall all the kindreds of the earth be blessed. Unto you first God, having raised up his Son Yeshua (Jesus), sent him to bless you, in turning every one of you away from his iniquities.'"*

This diptych painting is a scene showing the modern-day Mount of Olives (Olivet). It was done on two panels because one represents Jesus' ascension from this earth, and the other one for the day of His return. It also signifies what the scripture describes will happen on the day Jesus returns: *"And his feet shall stand that day on the mount of Olives, which is by Jerusalem on the east, and the mount of Olives will divide toward the east and the west and there will be a very great valley; and half of the mountain will move toward the north, and half of it toward the south . . . and the LORD my God shall come and all the saints with Him."*

©2017 His Ascension & His Return (Diptych)—Eternal Perspective: Connecting the Crimson Dots of His Covenant

WHO IS RETURNING?

When Jesus was still on the earth, he spoke of what was yet to come until all things written about were fulfilled and the times of the Gentiles were fulfilled. He said, *"And there will be signs in the sun and in the moon, and in the stars; and upon the earth distress of nations, with perplexity; the sea and the waves roaring; men's hearts failing them for fear, and for looking after these things which are coming on the earth: for the powers of heaven shall be shaken. And they will see the Son of man coming in a cloud with power and great glory. And when these things begin to come to pass, then look up, and lift up your heads; for your redemption draws near . . . when you see these things happen, know that the kingdom of God is near at hand . . . Heaven and earth shall pass away: but my words shall not pass away. And take heed to yourselves, should at any time your hearts be burdened with the headaches caused by drunkenness, and cares of this life, and so that day comes upon you unexpectedly. For as a snare it will come on all them that dwell on the face of the whole earth. Watch therefore, and always pray, that you may be accounted worthy to escape all these things that will come to pass, and to stand before the Son of man."* Luke 21:25–38 and Matthew 24:1–51 give many details about this event.

"Immediately after the tribulation of those days the sun will be darkened, and the moon will not give her light, and the stars will fall from heaven, and the powers of the heavens will be shaken. And then the sign of the Son of man will appear in heaven, and then all the tribes of the earth will mourn, and they will see the Son of man coming in the clouds of heaven with power and great glory. And he shall send his angels with a great sound of a trumpet, and they shall gather together his elect from the four winds, from one end of heaven to the other. Now learn a parable of the fig tree; when his branch is still tender, and puts forth leaves, you will know that summer is near. So likewise, when you will see all these things, know that it is near, even at the doors. Truly I say to you, this generation will not pass, until all these things are fulfilled. Heaven and earth will pass away, but my words will not pass away. But of that day and hour no man knows, no, not the angels of heaven, but my Father only. But just as the days of Noe (Noah in Greek) were, so shall the coming of the Son of man also be. For as in the days that were before the flood they were eating and drinking, marrying and giving in marriage, until the day that Noe entered into the ark, and did not know until the flood came, and took them all away; so also shall be the coming of the Son of man."

• The Apostle Paul documented in 1 Thessalonians 4:16–18, *"The Lord himself shall descend from heaven with a shout, with the voice of the archangel, and with the trump of God: and the dead in Christ shall rise first: then we which are alive and remain shall be caught up together with them in the clouds, and meet the Lord in the air: and so shall we ever be with the Lord. Wherefore comfort one another with these words."*

• *"But God gave it a body as it has pleased him, and to every seed his own body. All flesh is not the same flesh . . . So also is the resurrection of the dead. It is sown in corruption; it is raised in incorruption. It is sown in dishonor; it is raised in glory. It is sown in weakness; it is raised in power. It is sown in a natural body; it is raised a spiritual body. There is a natural body, and there is a spiritual body. And so it is written, 'The first man Adam was made a living soul; the last Adam (Yeshua) was made a quickening spirit. Nevertheless the first is natural and afterward is spiritual. The first man is of the earth, earthy; the second man is the Lord from heaven. As is the earthy, such are they also earthy: and as is the heavenly, such are they also heavenly. And as we have borne the image of the earthy, we will also bear the image of the heavenly.' Now this I say, brothers, that flesh and blood cannot inherit the kingdom of God; neither does corruption inherit incorruption. Behold, I show you a mystery; we will not all sleep (pass away), but we will all be changed, in a moment, in the twinkling of an eye, at the last trump. For the trumpet will sound, and the dead will be raised incorruptible, and we will be changed. For this corruptible must put on incorruption, and this mortal must put on immortality. So when this corruptible will have put on incorruption, and this mortal will have put on immortality, then it shall be brought to pass the saying that it is written, 'Death is swallowed up in victory. Oh death, where is your sting? Oh grave, where is your victory? The sting of death is sin; and the strength of sin is the law. But thanks be to God, which gives us the victory through our Lord Jesus Christ. Therefore, my beloved brothers, be steadfast, unmovable, always abounding in the work of the Lord, for as much as you know that your labor is not in vain in the Lord."* See also 1 Thessalonians 5:1–18.

• *"And for this cause he is the mediator of the new testament (covenant), that by means of death, for the redemption of the transgressions that were under the first testament, they which are called might receive the promise of **eternal inheritance.**"* Jesus came to take away the first, to establish the second which sanctifies us through the offering of his body once for all (Hebrews 9:15).

• *"And it is appointed for men to die once, but after this the judgment. So Christ was offered once to bear the sins of many; and to those that look for him, he will appear the second time without sin to salvation."* This is recorded in Hebrews 9:27–28.

IS IT TIME TO REMOVE THE IDOLS?

Are you ready for what is about to take place on the earth? Do you know where your eternal habitation will be? You can know with certainty how to live in eternity with your Creator if you so choose. *"Those who call upon the Lord shall be saved."* Today is the day of salvation. Researching all of this deeper, you will find theologians who differ on the timing of Jesus' return. One thing I can assure you of is that when you leave this exhibit, it is up to you to choose. Our Creator does not force anyone to be with Him for eternity. He wants us to freely love Him and choose Him. None of us knows the moment when our physical time on earth will expire and our eternal state will continue in the spirit.

• Historical records and ancient scriptures document the cycle of idolatry that occurred. Recorded in 1 Kings 19:9 through the end of 2 Kings, it is written that the King of Assyria carried Israel away *"Because they did not obey the voice of the LORD their God, but transgressed his covenant, and all that Moses the servant of the LORD commanded, and would not hear them, nor do them."*

• Zechariah 10:2–3 records, *"For the idols have spoken vanity, and the diviners have seen a lie, and they have told false dreams. They comfort in vain, therefore they went their way as a flock. They were troubled because there was no shepherd. My anger was kindled against the shepherds, and I punished the goats, for the LORD of hosts has* **visited** *his flock of the house of Judah, and has made them as his goodly (Strong's #1935 describes this as grandest beauty, comliness, excellency, glorious, glory, honor and majesty) horse in battle."*

• The apostle Paul declared to an audience in Acts 17:24–31, *"God that made the world and all things therein, seeing that he is Lord of heaven and earth, dwells not in temples made with hands. Neither is worshipped with men's hands, as though he needed anything, seeing he gives to all life, and breath, and all things. And has made of one blood all nations of men to dwell on all the face of the earth, and has determined the times before appointed, and the bounds of their habitation; that they should seek the Lord, if they treasure him, and find him, though he is not far from every one of us. For in him we live, and move, and have our being, as certain also of your own poets have said, For we are also his offspring. Forasmuch then as we are the offspring of God, we ought not to think that the Godhead is like unto gold, or silver, or stone, graven by art and man's device. And the times of this ignorance God did not punish; but now commands all men everywhere to repent, because he has appointed a day, in which he will judge the world in righteousness by that man who he has ordained. Whereof he has given assurance to all men, in that he has raised him from the dead."*

Isaiah 55:6–7 says, *"Seek the LORD while he may be found. Call upon him while he is near. Let the wicked forsake his way, and the unrighteous man his thoughts, and let him return to the LORD, and to our God, and he will have mercy on him. For he will abundantly pardon."*

This painting is from a location known as a high place. In 1 and 2 Chronicles and 1 and 2 Kings we read that there were both good kings and kings that did evil in God's eyes, and it would say many times that they did not remove the high places. I finally understood what that phrase meant when we visited this location.

©2017 Removing The High Places—Eternal Perspective: Connecting the Crimson Dots of His Covenant

WHAT WILL THE EARTH LOOK LIKE WHEN ALL THINGS ARE RESTORED?

Before the earth is restored to the state originally intended for us by our Creator, there are several more prophecies that many feel are yet to be fulfilled. One is known as the final battle on the earth in a location called Armageddon (Megiddo). The top panel is a scene yet to come based on Matthew 24:29–31, 1 Corinthians 15:51–52, Revelation 16:15–16, and 11:15–19 (seventh of seven trumpets). The middle and bottom panels of this triptych are a scene from a site overlooking the valley that contains Megiddo in the distance.

• 1 Corinthians 15:20–58, written circa 59 AD by the Apostle Paul, says, *"But now Christ has risen from the dead, and has become the first fruits of them that slept (passed away). For since by man came death, by man came also the resurrection of the dead. For as in Adam all die, even so in Christ (Messiah) shall all be made alive. But every man in his own order: Christ the first fruits; afterward they that are Christ's at his coming. Then comes the end, when he will have delivered up the kingdom to God, even the Father; when he will have put down all rule and all authority and power. For he must reign, until he has put all enemies under his feet. The last enemy that shall be destroyed is death. For he has put all things under his feet. But when he says all things are put under him, it is manifest that he is excepted, which did put all things under him. And when all things shall be subdued to him, then shall the Son also himself be subject to him that puts all things under him, that God may be all in all . . ."*

• *"And the LORD shall be king over all the earth: in that day there shall be one LORD, and his name one"* (Zechariah 14:9).

• The book of Revelation speaks about the restitution of all things and reveals past, present, and future events that are continually unfolding on earth. It takes us through a series of visions that the apostle John was shown taking place in the spiritual realm that describe seven seals being opened, seven trumpets being sounded, and seven vials being poured out. Revelation 5:1—7:17 describes that no one was found worthy to open the book containing the seven seals until Yeshua (Jesus) the Lamb of God was found worthy. It goes on to describe that after the seals were opened, the trumpets would sound, with the final one concluding the finished work. In Revelation 11:15 it is written, *"And the seventh angel sounded; and there were great voices in heaven, saying, the kingdoms of this world are becoming the kingdoms of our Lord, and of his Christ; and he shall reign for ever and ever."*

©2017 His Final Victory (Triptych)—Eternal Perspective: Connecting the Crimson Dots of His Covenant

• In the book of Daniel, many visions shown to him for the time of the end are recorded. The last chapter reveals, *"And at that time shall Michael stand up, the great prince which stands for the children of your people, and there shall be a time of trouble, such as never was since there was a nation even to that same time. And at that time your people shall be delivered,* **every one that should be found written in the book.** *And many of them that sleep in the dust of the earth shall awake, some to everlasting life, and some to shame and everlasting contempt. And they that are wise shall shine as the brightness of the firmament; and they that turn many to righteousness as the stars for ever and ever. But you, Daniel, shut up the words, and seal the book, even to the time of the end. Many will run to and fro, and knowledge shall be increased . . . 'How long shall it be to the end of these wonders?' . . . And he said 'Go your way Daniel: for the words are closed up and sealed until the time of the end. Many shall be purified, and made white, and tried; but the wicked shall do wickedly. And none of the wicked shall understand; but the wise shall understand. And from the time that the daily sacrifice shall be taken away, and the abomination that makes it desolate is set up, there shall be a thousand two hundred and ninety days. Blessed is he that waits, and comes to the thousand three hundred and thirty-five days. But go your way until the end will be, for you shall rest (die), and stand in your lot at the end of the days.'"*

• This final battle will be led by Yeshua's (Jesus') physical return to earth with his raised and glorified armies as revealed to John in a vision recorded in Revelation 19:11–16. *"And I saw heaven opened and behold a white horse; and he that sat upon him was called Faithful and TRUE, and in righteousness he does judge and make war. His eyes were as a flame of fire, and on his head were many crowns; and he had a name written that no man knew, but he himself. And he was clothed with a vesture dipped in blood: and his name is called 'The WORD of God.' And the armies which were in heaven followed him on white horses, clothed in fine linen, white and clean. And out of his mouth goes a sharp sword, that with it he will rule them with a rod of iron: and he treads the winepress of the fierceness and wrath of Almighty God. And he had on his vesture and on his thigh a name written, KING OF KINGS, AND LORD OF LORDS."*

This battle will be followed by a 1,000 year reign with Yeshua (Jesus) ruling the earth during a time when the deceiver and enemy of our souls and evil is bound. This is recorded in Revelation 20:1–3: *"And I saw an angel come down from heaven, having a key of the bottomless pit and a great chain in his hand. And he laid hold of the dragon, that old serpent, which is the Devil, and Satan, and bound him a thousand years, and cast him into the bottomless pit, and shut him up, and set a seal on him, that he should deceive the nations no more, until the thousand years should be fulfilled. And after that he must be loosed a little season."*

After the 1,000 year reign, the deceiver will be unbound, and souls living in the millennium will choose their eternal destiny. They can opt to live in the midst of God our Creator forever or rebel and reject our

Creator God and follow the deceiver. There will be a time of final judgment for all who have walked this earth. Revelation 20:1–15 documents this part of the story.

Then the earth will again be restored to what our Creator intended for us to inhabit from the beginning, filled with "the fruit of the Spirit which is love, joy, peace, long suffering, gentleness, faith, meekness and temperance." The deceiver and those choosing to follow him, will then meet their eternal destiny, which will be apart from God forever in a state of torment.

Did you know that one day with our Creator is as a thousand years? And that He *"is not slack concerning his promise . . . but is long suffering toward us, not willing that any should perish, but that all would come to repentance."* This is recorded in 2 Peter 3:8–9.

• Several prophesies have been fulfilled in this past century. One partially fulfilled in 1948 was that the Israelites would be gathered from among all the countries and brought back into their own land. Ezekiel 36:1–37:28 records, *"And say to them, Thus says the Lord God: Behold, I will take the children of Israel from among the Gentiles, where they have gone, and will gather them on every side, and bring them into their own land. And I will make them one nation in the land on the mountains of Israel; and one king shall be king to them all. And they shall no more be two nations, neither shall they be divided into two kingdoms.* Earlier the LORD God said, *"A new heart also will I give you: and I will take away the stony heart out of your flesh. And I will put my SPIRIT within you, and cause you to walk in my statutes, and you shall keep my judgements, and do them. And you shall dwell in the land that I gave your fathers; and you shall be my people, and I will be your God …Moreover I will make a* covenant *of peace with them; it shall be an* everlasting covenant *with them: and I will place them, and multiply them, and will set my sanctuary in the midst of them forever more."*

• Earlier in the story, after Jesus ascended, his disciple Peter healed a lame man and *"answered to the people, 'You men of Israel why do you marvel at this, or look so earnestly at us, as though by our own power or holiness we made this man walk? The God of Abraham, Isaac, and Jacob, the God of our fathers, has glorified his Son Jesus; who you delivered up, denied him in the presence of Pilate, when he was determined to let him go. But you denied the Holy One and the Just, and desired a murderer to be granted unto you; and killed the Prince of LIFE, whom God has raised from the dead; whereof we are witnesses. And his name through faith in his name has made this man strong, whom you see and know. Yes, the faith which is by him has given him this perfect soundness in the presence of you all. And now, brothers, I understand that through your ignorance you did it, as your rulers also did. But these things, which God before had shown by the mouth of all his prophets, that Christ should suffer, he has so fulfilled. Repent then, and be converted, that your sins may be blotted out, when the times of refreshing shall come from the presence of the Lord'"* (Acts 3:11–26). Look up Matthew

13:36–52 to read what Jesus had to say about the end of the story.

It is written in Romans 1:20–22 that "*For the invisible things of God from the creation of the world are clearly seen, being understood by the things that are made, even his eternal power and Godhead; so that they are without excuse, because that, when they knew God, they did not glorify him as God, neither were they thankful; but became vain in their imaginations, and their foolish heart was darkened. Professing themselves to be wise, they became fools, and changed the glory of the uncorruptible God into an image made like corruptible man, and to birds, and four-footed beasts, and creeping things. Therefore God also gave them up to uncleanness through the lusts of their own hearts, to dishonor their own bodies between themselves, who changed the truth of God into a lie, and worshipped and served the creature more than the Creator who is blessed forever. Amen.*"

"*Come now, and let us reason together, says the LORD: though your sins (offenses) be as scarlet, they will be as white as snow; though they be red like crimson, they shall be as wool. If you are willing and obedient, you shall eat the good of the land. But if you refuse and rebel, you shall be devoured with the sword: for the mouth of the LORD has spoken it.*" This was recorded in Isaiah 1:18–20.

The last book of Revelation documents "*. . . And he said to me, seal not the sayings of the prophecy of this book: for the time is at hand . . .*"

Is your name written in the Lamb's Book of Life? See Revelation 20:12–15. The entire book of Revelation is included so that you can read it for yourself. Ask God to give you His revelation by the power of the Holy Spirit. I encourage you to do your own research to authenticate the answers.

• I pray "*That the God of our Lord Jesus Christ, the Father of glory, may give you the spirit of wisdom and revelation in the knowledge of him: the eyes of your understanding being enlightened; that you may know what is the HOPE of his calling, and what the riches of the glory of his **inheritance** in the saints and what is the exceeding greatness of His power toward us who believe, according to the working of his mighty power which he worked in Christ, when he raised him from the dead, and set him at his own right hand in the heavenly places, far above all principality, and power, and might, and dominion, and every name that is named, not only in this world, but also in that which is to come. And has put all things under his feet, and gave him to be the head over all things to the church, which is his body, the fulness of him that fills all in all,*" (Ephesians 1:17–23).

Revelation
King James Version (KJV)

1 The Revelation of Jesus Christ, which God gave unto him, to shew unto his servants things which must shortly come to pass; and he sent and signified it by his angel unto his servant John:

² Who bare record of the word of God, and of the testimony of Jesus Christ, and of all things that he saw.

³ Blessed is he that readeth, and they that hear the words of this prophecy, and keep those things which are written therein: for the time is at hand.

⁴ John to the seven churches which are in Asia: Grace be unto you, and peace, from him which is, and which was, and which is to come; and from the seven Spirits which are before his throne;

⁵ And from Jesus Christ, who is the faithful witness, and the first begotten of the dead, and the prince of the kings of the earth. Unto him that loved us, and washed us from our sins in his own blood,

⁶ And hath made us kings and priests unto God and his Father; to him be glory and dominion for ever and ever. Amen.

⁷ Behold, he cometh with clouds; and every eye shall see him, and they also which pierced him: and all kindreds of the earth shall wail because of him. Even so, Amen.

⁸ I am Alpha and Omega, the beginning and the ending, saith the Lord, which is, and which was, and which is to come, the Almighty.

⁹ I John, who also am your brother, and companion in tribulation, and in the kingdom and patience of Jesus Christ, was in the isle that is called Patmos, for the word of God, and for the testimony of Jesus Christ.

¹⁰ I was in the Spirit on the Lord's day, and heard behind me a great voice, as of a trumpet,

¹¹ Saying, I am Alpha and Omega, the first and the last: and, What thou seest, write in a book, and send it unto the seven churches which are in Asia; unto Ephesus, and unto Smyrna, and unto Pergamos, and unto Thyatira, and unto Sardis, and unto Philadelphia, and unto Laodicea.

¹² And I turned to see the voice that spake with me. And being turned, I saw seven golden candlesticks;

¹³ And in the midst of the seven candlesticks one like unto the Son of man, clothed with a garment down to the foot, and girt about the paps with a golden girdle.

[14] His head and his hairs were white like wool, as white as snow; and his eyes were as a flame of fire;

[15] And his feet like unto fine brass, as if they burned in a furnace; and his voice as the sound of many waters.

[16] And he had in his right hand seven stars: and out of his mouth went a sharp twoedged sword: and his countenance was as the sun shineth in his strength.

[17] And when I saw him, I fell at his feet as dead. And he laid his right hand upon me, saying unto me, Fear not; I am the first and the last:

[18] I am he that liveth, and was dead; and, behold, I am alive for evermore, Amen; and have the keys of hell and of death.

[19] Write the things which thou hast seen, and the things which are, and the things which shall be hereafter;

[20] The mystery of the seven stars which thou sawest in my right hand, and the seven golden candlesticks. The seven stars are the angels of the seven churches: and the seven candlesticks which thou sawest are the seven churches.

2 Unto the angel of the church of Ephesus write; These things saith he that holdeth the seven stars in his right hand, who walketh in the midst of the seven golden candlesticks;

[2] I know thy works, and thy labour, and thy patience, and how thou canst not bear them which are evil: and thou hast tried them which say they are apostles, and are not, and hast found them liars:

[3] And hast borne, and hast patience, and for my name's sake hast laboured, and hast not fainted.

[4] Nevertheless I have somewhat against thee, because thou hast left thy first love.

[5] Remember therefore from whence thou art fallen, and repent, and do the first works; or else I will come unto thee quickly, and will remove thy candlestick out of his place, except thou repent.

[6] But this thou hast, that thou hatest the deeds of the Nicolaitanes, which I also hate.

[7] He that hath an ear, let him hear what the Spirit saith unto the churches; To him that overcometh will I give to eat of the tree of life, which is in the midst of the paradise of God.

[8] And unto the angel of the church in Smyrna write; These things saith the first and the last, which was dead, and is alive;

[9] I know thy works, and tribulation, and poverty, (but thou art rich) and I know the blasphemy of them which say they are Jews, and are not, but are the synagogue of Satan.

¹⁰ Fear none of those things which thou shalt suffer: behold, the devil shall cast some of you into prison, that ye may be tried; and ye shall have tribulation ten days: be thou faithful unto death, and I will give thee a crown of life.

¹¹ He that hath an ear, let him hear what the Spirit saith unto the churches; He that overcometh shall not be hurt of the second death.

¹² And to the angel of the church in Pergamos write; These things saith he which hath the sharp sword with two edges;

¹³ I know thy works, and where thou dwellest, even where Satan's seat is: and thou holdest fast my name, and hast not denied my faith, even in those days wherein Antipas was my faithful martyr, who was slain among you, where Satan dwelleth.

¹⁴ But I have a few things against thee, because thou hast there them that hold the doctrine of Balaam, who taught Balac to cast a stumblingblock before the children of Israel, to eat things sacrificed unto idols, and to commit fornication.

¹⁵ So hast thou also them that hold the doctrine of the Nicolaitanes, which thing I hate.

¹⁶ Repent; or else I will come unto thee quickly, and will fight against them with the sword of my mouth.

¹⁷ He that hath an ear, let him hear what the Spirit saith unto the churches; To him that overcometh will I give to eat of the hidden manna, and will give him a white stone, and in the stone a new name written, which no man knoweth saving he that receiveth it.

¹⁸ And unto the angel of the church in Thyatira write; These things saith the Son of God, who hath his eyes like unto a flame of fire, and his feet are like fine brass;

¹⁹ I know thy works, and charity, and service, and faith, and thy patience, and thy works; and the last to be more than the first.

²⁰ Notwithstanding I have a few things against thee, because thou sufferest that woman Jezebel, which calleth herself a prophetess, to teach and to seduce my servants to commit fornication, and to eat things sacrificed unto idols.

²¹ And I gave her space to repent of her fornication; and she repented not.

²² Behold, I will cast her into a bed, and them that commit adultery with her into great tribulation, except they repent of their deeds.

²³ And I will kill her children with death; and all the churches shall know that I am he which searcheth the reins and hearts: and I will give unto every one of you according to your works.

²⁴ But unto you I say, and unto the rest in Thyatira, as many as have not this doctrine, and which have not known the depths of Satan, as they speak; I will put upon you none other burden.

²⁵ But that which ye have already hold fast till I come.

²⁶ And he that overcometh, and keepeth my works unto the end, to him will I give power over the nations:

²⁷ And he shall rule them with a rod of iron; as the vessels of a potter shall they be broken to shivers: even as I received of my Father.

²⁸ And I will give him the morning star.

²⁹ He that hath an ear, let him hear what the Spirit saith unto the churches.

3 And unto the angel of the church in Sardis write; These things saith he that hath the seven Spirits of God, and the seven stars; I know thy works, that thou hast a name that thou livest, and art dead.

² Be watchful, and strengthen the things which remain, that are ready to die: for I have not found thy works perfect before God.

³ Remember therefore how thou hast received and heard, and hold fast, and repent. If therefore thou shalt not watch, I will come on thee as a thief, and thou shalt not know what hour I will come upon thee.

⁴ Thou hast a few names even in Sardis which have not defiled their garments; and they shall walk with me in white: for they are worthy.

⁵ He that overcometh, the same shall be clothed in white raiment; and I will not blot out his name out of the book of life, but I will confess his name before my Father, and before his angels.

⁶ He that hath an ear, let him hear what the Spirit saith unto the churches.

⁷ And to the angel of the church in Philadelphia write; These things saith he that is holy, he that is true, he that hath the key of David, he that openeth, and no man shutteth; and shutteth, and no man openeth;

⁸ I know thy works: behold, I have set before thee an open door, and no man can shut it: for thou hast a little strength, and hast kept my word, and hast not denied my name.

⁹ Behold, I will make them of the synagogue of Satan, which say they are Jews, and are not, but do lie; behold, I will make them to come and worship before thy feet, and to know that I have loved thee.

¹⁰ Because thou hast kept the word of my patience, I also will keep thee from the hour of temptation, which shall come upon all the world, to try them that dwell upon the earth.

¹¹ Behold, I come quickly: hold that fast which thou hast, that no man take thy crown.

[12] Him that overcometh will I make a pillar in the temple of my God, and he shall go no more out: and I will write upon him the name of my God, and the name of the city of my God, which is new Jerusalem, which cometh down out of heaven from my God: and I will write upon him my new name.

[13] He that hath an ear, let him hear what the Spirit saith unto the churches.

[14] And unto the angel of the church of the Laodiceans write; These things saith the Amen, the faithful and true witness, the beginning of the creation of God;

[15] I know thy works, that thou art neither cold nor hot: I would thou wert cold or hot.

[16] So then because thou art lukewarm, and neither cold nor hot, I will spue thee out of my mouth.

[17] Because thou sayest, I am rich, and increased with goods, and have need of nothing; and knowest not that thou art wretched, and miserable, and poor, and blind, and naked:

[18] I counsel thee to buy of me gold tried in the fire, that thou mayest be rich; and white raiment, that thou mayest be clothed, and that the shame of thy nakedness do not appear; and anoint thine eyes with eyesalve, that thou mayest see.

[19] As many as I love, I rebuke and chasten: be zealous therefore, and repent.

[20] Behold, I stand at the door, and knock: if any man hear my voice, and open the door, I will come in to him, and will sup with him, and he with me.

[21] To him that overcometh will I grant to sit with me in my throne, even as I also overcame, and am set down with my Father in his throne.

[22] He that hath an ear, let him hear what the Spirit saith unto the churches.

4 After this I looked, and, behold, a door was opened in heaven: and the first voice which I heard was as it were of a trumpet talking with me; which said, Come up hither, and I will shew thee things which must be hereafter.

[2] And immediately I was in the spirit: and, behold, a throne was set in heaven, and one sat on the throne.

[3] And he that sat was to look upon like a jasper and a sardine stone: and there was a rainbow round about the throne, in sight like unto an emerald.

[4] And round about the throne were four and twenty seats: and upon the seats I saw four and twenty elders sitting, clothed in white raiment; and they had on their heads crowns of gold.

[5] And out of the throne proceeded lightnings and thunderings and voices: and there were seven lamps

of fire burning before the throne, which are the seven Spirits of God.

⁶ And before the throne there was a sea of glass like unto crystal: and in the midst of the throne, and round about the throne, were four beasts full of eyes before and behind.

⁷ And the first beast was like a lion, and the second beast like a calf, and the third beast had a face as a man, and the fourth beast was like a flying eagle.

⁸ And the four beasts had each of them six wings about him; and they were full of eyes within: and they rest not day and night, saying, Holy, holy, holy, LORD God Almighty, which was, and is, and is to come.

⁹ And when those beasts give glory and honour and thanks to him that sat on the throne, who liveth for ever and ever,

¹⁰ The four and twenty elders fall down before him that sat on the throne, and worship him that liveth for ever and ever, and cast their crowns before the throne, saying,

¹¹ Thou art worthy, O Lord, to receive glory and honour and power: for thou hast created all things, and for thy pleasure they are and were created.

5 And I saw in the right hand of him that sat on the throne a book written within and on the backside, sealed with seven seals.

² And I saw a strong angel proclaiming with a loud voice, Who is worthy to open the book, and to loose the seals thereof?

³ And no man in heaven, nor in earth, neither under the earth, was able to open the book, neither to look thereon.

⁴ And I wept much, because no man was found worthy to open and to read the book, neither to look thereon.

⁵ And one of the elders saith unto me, Weep not: behold, the Lion of the tribe of Judah, the Root of David, hath prevailed to open the book, and to loose the seven seals thereof.

⁶ And I beheld, and, lo, in the midst of the throne and of the four beasts, and in the midst of the elders, stood a Lamb as it had been slain, having seven horns and seven eyes, which are the seven Spirits of God sent forth into all the earth.

⁷ And he came and took the book out of the right hand of him that sat upon the throne.

⁸ And when he had taken the book, the four beasts and four and twenty elders fell down before the

Lamb, having every one of them harps, and golden vials full of odours, which are the prayers of saints.

⁹ And they sung a new song, saying, Thou art worthy to take the book, and to open the seals thereof: for thou wast slain, and hast redeemed us to God by thy blood out of every kindred, and tongue, and people, and nation;

¹⁰ And hast made us unto our God kings and priests: and we shall reign on the earth.

¹¹ And I beheld, and I heard the voice of many angels round about the throne and the beasts and the elders: and the number of them was ten thousand times ten thousand, and thousands of thousands;

¹² Saying with a loud voice, Worthy is the Lamb that was slain to receive power, and riches, and wisdom, and strength, and honour, and glory, and blessing.

¹³ And every creature which is in heaven, and on the earth, and under the earth, and such as are in the sea, and all that are in them, heard I saying, Blessing, and honour, and glory, and power, be unto him that sitteth upon the throne, and unto the Lamb for ever and ever.

¹⁴ And the four beasts said, Amen. And the four and twenty elders fell down and worshipped him that liveth for ever and ever.

6 And I saw when the Lamb opened one of the seals, and I heard, as it were the noise of thunder, one of the four beasts saying, Come and see.

² And I saw, and behold a white horse: and he that sat on him had a bow; and a crown was given unto him: and he went forth conquering, and to conquer.

³ And when he had opened the second seal, I heard the second beast say, Come and see.

⁴ And there went out another horse that was red: and power was given to him that sat thereon to take peace from the earth, and that they should kill one another: and there was given unto him a great sword.

⁵ And when he had opened the third seal, I heard the third beast say, Come and see. And I beheld, and lo a black horse; and he that sat on him had a pair of balances in his hand.

⁶ And I heard a voice in the midst of the four beasts say, A measure of wheat for a penny, and three measures of barley for a penny; and see thou hurt not the oil and the wine.

⁷ And when he had opened the fourth seal, I heard the voice of the fourth beast say, Come and see.

⁸ And I looked, and behold a pale horse: and his name that sat on him was Death, and Hell followed with him. And power was given unto them over the fourth part of the earth, to kill with sword, and with hunger, and with death, and with the beasts of the earth.

[9] And when he had opened the fifth seal, I saw under the altar the souls of them that were slain for the word of God, and for the testimony which they held:

[10] And they cried with a loud voice, saying, How long, O Lord, holy and true, dost thou not judge and avenge our blood on them that dwell on the earth?

[11] And white robes were given unto every one of them; and it was said unto them, that they should rest yet for a little season, until their fellowservants also and their brethren, that should be killed as they were, should be fulfilled.

[12] And I beheld when he had opened the sixth seal, and, lo, there was a great earthquake; and the sun became black as sackcloth of hair, and the moon became as blood;

[13] And the stars of heaven fell unto the earth, even as a fig tree casteth her untimely figs, when she is shaken of a mighty wind.

[14] And the heaven departed as a scroll when it is rolled together; and every mountain and island were moved out of their places.

[15] And the kings of the earth, and the great men, and the rich men, and the chief captains, and the mighty men, and every bondman, and every free man, hid themselves in the dens and in the rocks of the mountains;

[16] And said to the mountains and rocks, Fall on us, and hide us from the face of him that sitteth on the throne, and from the wrath of the Lamb:

[17] For the great day of his wrath is come; and who shall be able to stand?

7 And after these things I saw four angels standing on the four corners of the earth, holding the four winds of the earth, that the wind should not blow on the earth, nor on the sea, nor on any tree.

[2] And I saw another angel ascending from the east, having the seal of the living God: and he cried with a loud voice to the four angels, to whom it was given to hurt the earth and the sea,

[3] Saying, Hurt not the earth, neither the sea, nor the trees, till we have sealed the servants of our God in their foreheads.

[4] And I heard the number of them which were sealed: and there were sealed an hundred and forty and four thousand of all the tribes of the children of Israel.

[5] Of the tribe of Juda were sealed twelve thousand. Of the tribe of Reuben were sealed twelve thousand. Of the tribe of Gad were sealed twelve thousand.

⁶ Of the tribe of Aser were sealed twelve thousand. Of the tribe of Nephthalim were sealed twelve thousand. Of the tribe of Manasses were sealed twelve thousand.

⁷ Of the tribe of Simeon were sealed twelve thousand. Of the tribe of Levi were sealed twelve thousand. Of the tribe of Issachar were sealed twelve thousand.

⁸ Of the tribe of Zabulon were sealed twelve thousand. Of the tribe of Joseph were sealed twelve thousand. Of the tribe of Benjamin were sealed twelve thousand.

⁹ After this I beheld, and, lo, a great multitude, which no man could number, of all nations, and kindreds, and people, and tongues, stood before the throne, and before the Lamb, clothed with white robes, and palms in their hands;

¹⁰ And cried with a loud voice, saying, Salvation to our God which sitteth upon the throne, and unto the Lamb.

¹¹ And all the angels stood round about the throne, and about the elders and the four beasts, and fell before the throne on their faces, and worshipped God,

¹² Saying, Amen: Blessing, and glory, and wisdom, and thanksgiving, and honour, and power, and might, be unto our God for ever and ever. Amen.

¹³ And one of the elders answered, saying unto me, What are these which are arrayed in white robes? and whence came they?

¹⁴ And I said unto him, Sir, thou knowest. And he said to me, These are they which came out of great tribulation, and have washed their robes, and made them white in the blood of the Lamb.

¹⁵ Therefore are they before the throne of God, and serve him day and night in his temple: and he that sitteth on the throne shall dwell among them.

¹⁶ They shall hunger no more, neither thirst any more; neither shall the sun light on them, nor any heat.

¹⁷ For the Lamb which is in the midst of the throne shall feed them, and shall lead them unto living fountains of waters: and God shall wipe away all tears from their eyes.

8 And when he had opened the seventh seal, there was silence in heaven about the space of half an hour.

² And I saw the seven angels which stood before God; and to them were given seven trumpets.

³ And another angel came and stood at the altar, having a golden censer; and there was given unto him

much incense, that he should offer it with the prayers of all saints upon the golden altar which was before the throne.

⁴ And the smoke of the incense, which came with the prayers of the saints, ascended up before God out of the angel's hand.

⁵ And the angel took the censer, and filled it with fire of the altar, and cast it into the earth: and there were voices, and thunderings, and lightnings, and an earthquake.

⁶ And the seven angels which had the seven trumpets prepared themselves to sound.

⁷ The first angel sounded, and there followed hail and fire mingled with blood, and they were cast upon the earth: and the third part of trees was burnt up, and all green grass was burnt up.

⁸ And the second angel sounded, and as it were a great mountain burning with fire was cast into the sea: and the third part of the sea became blood;

⁹ And the third part of the creatures which were in the sea, and had life, died; and the third part of the ships were destroyed.

¹⁰ And the third angel sounded, and there fell a great star from heaven, burning as it were a lamp, and it fell upon the third part of the rivers, and upon the fountains of waters;

¹¹ And the name of the star is called Wormwood: and the third part of the waters became wormwood; and many men died of the waters, because they were made bitter.

¹² And the fourth angel sounded, and the third part of the sun was smitten, and the third part of the moon, and the third part of the stars; so as the third part of them was darkened, and the day shone not for a third part of it, and the night likewise.

¹³ And I beheld, and heard an angel flying through the midst of heaven, saying with a loud voice, Woe, woe, woe, to the inhabiters of the earth by reason of the other voices of the trumpet of the three angels, which are yet to sound!

9 And the fifth angel sounded, and I saw a star fall from heaven unto the earth: and to him was given the key of the bottomless pit.

² And he opened the bottomless pit; and there arose a smoke out of the pit, as the smoke of a great furnace; and the sun and the air were darkened by reason of the smoke of the pit.

³ And there came out of the smoke locusts upon the earth: and unto them was given power, as the scorpions of the earth have power.

⁴ And it was commanded them that they should not hurt the grass of the earth, neither any green

thing, neither any tree; but only those men which have not the seal of God in their foreheads.

⁵ And to them it was given that they should not kill them, but that they should be tormented five months: and their torment was as the torment of a scorpion, when he striketh a man.

⁶ And in those days shall men seek death, and shall not find it; and shall desire to die, and death shall flee from them.

⁷ And the shapes of the locusts were like unto horses prepared unto battle; and on their heads were as it were crowns like gold, and their faces were as the faces of men.

⁸ And they had hair as the hair of women, and their teeth were as the teeth of lions.

⁹ And they had breastplates, as it were breastplates of iron; and the sound of their wings was as the sound of chariots of many horses running to battle.

¹⁰ And they had tails like unto scorpions, and there were stings in their tails: and their power was to hurt men five months.

¹¹ And they had a king over them, which is the angel of the bottomless pit, whose name in the Hebrew tongue is Abaddon, but in the Greek tongue hath his name Apollyon.

¹² One woe is past; and, behold, there come two woes more hereafter.

¹³ And the sixth angel sounded, and I heard a voice from the four horns of the golden altar which is before God,

¹⁴ Saying to the sixth angel which had the trumpet, Loose the four angels which are bound in the great river Euphrates.

¹⁵ And the four angels were loosed, which were prepared for an hour, and a day, and a month, and a year, for to slay the third part of men.

¹⁶ And the number of the army of the horsemen were two hundred thousand thousand: and I heard the number of them.

¹⁷ And thus I saw the horses in the vision, and them that sat on them, having breastplates of fire, and of jacinth, and brimstone: and the heads of the horses were as the heads of lions; and out of their mouths issued fire and smoke and brimstone.

¹⁸ By these three was the third part of men killed, by the fire, and by the smoke, and by the brimstone, which issued out of their mouths.

¹⁹ For their power is in their mouth, and in their tails: for their tails were like unto serpents, and had heads, and with them they do hurt.

²⁰ And the rest of the men which were not killed by these plagues yet repented not of the works of

their hands, that they should not worship devils, and idols of gold, and silver, and brass, and stone, and of wood: which neither can see, nor hear, nor walk:

²¹ Neither repented they of their murders, nor of their sorceries, nor of their fornication, nor of their thefts.

10 And I saw another mighty angel come down from heaven, clothed with a cloud: and a rainbow was upon his head, and his face was as it were the sun, and his feet as pillars of fire:

² And he had in his hand a little book open: and he set his right foot upon the sea, and his left foot on the earth,

³ And cried with a loud voice, as when a lion roareth: and when he had cried, seven thunders uttered their voices.

⁴ And when the seven thunders had uttered their voices, I was about to write: and I heard a voice from heaven saying unto me, Seal up those things which the seven thunders uttered, and write them not.

⁵ And the angel which I saw stand upon the sea and upon the earth lifted up his hand to heaven,

⁶ And sware by him that liveth for ever and ever, who created heaven, and the things that therein are, and the earth, and the things that therein are, and the sea, and the things which are therein, that there should be time no longer:

⁷ But in the days of the voice of the seventh angel, when he shall begin to sound, the mystery of God should be finished, as he hath declared to his servants the prophets.

⁸ And the voice which I heard from heaven spake unto me again, and said, Go and take the little book which is open in the hand of the angel which standeth upon the sea and upon the earth.

⁹ And I went unto the angel, and said unto him, Give me the little book. And he said unto me, Take it, and eat it up; and it shall make thy belly bitter, but it shall be in thy mouth sweet as honey.

¹⁰ And I took the little book out of the angel's hand, and ate it up; and it was in my mouth sweet as honey: and as soon as I had eaten it, my belly was bitter.

¹¹ And he said unto me, Thou must prophesy again before many peoples, and nations, and tongues, and kings.

11 And there was given me a reed like unto a rod: and the angel stood, saying, Rise, and measure the temple of God, and the altar, and them that worship therein.

² But the court which is without the temple leave out, and measure it not; for it is given unto the Gentiles: and the holy city shall they tread under foot forty and two months.

³ And I will give power unto my two witnesses, and they shall prophesy a thousand two hundred and threescore days, clothed in sackcloth.

⁴ These are the two olive trees, and the two candlesticks standing before the God of the earth.

⁵ And if any man will hurt them, fire proceedeth out of their mouth, and devoureth their enemies: and if any man will hurt them, he must in this manner be killed.

⁶ These have power to shut heaven, that it rain not in the days of their prophecy: and have power over waters to turn them to blood, and to smite the earth with all plagues, as often as they will.

⁷ And when they shall have finished their testimony, the beast that ascendeth out of the bottomless pit shall make war against them, and shall overcome them, and kill them.

⁸ And their dead bodies shall lie in the street of the great city, which spiritually is called Sodom and Egypt, where also our Lord was crucified.

⁹ And they of the people and kindreds and tongues and nations shall see their dead bodies three days and an half, and shall not suffer their dead bodies to be put in graves.

¹⁰ And they that dwell upon the earth shall rejoice over them, and make merry, and shall send gifts one to another; because these two prophets tormented them that dwelt on the earth.

¹¹ And after three days and an half the spirit of life from God entered into them, and they stood upon their feet; and great fear fell upon them which saw them.

¹² And they heard a great voice from heaven saying unto them, Come up hither. And they ascended up to heaven in a cloud; and their enemies beheld them.

¹³ And the same hour was there a great earthquake, and the tenth part of the city fell, and in the earthquake were slain of men seven thousand: and the remnant were affrighted, and gave glory to the God of heaven.

¹⁴ The second woe is past; and, behold, the third woe cometh quickly.

¹⁵ And the seventh angel sounded; and there were great voices in heaven, saying, The kingdoms of this world are become the kingdoms of our Lord, and of his Christ; and he shall reign for ever and ever.

¹⁶ And the four and twenty elders, which sat before God on their seats, fell upon their faces, and worshipped God,

¹⁷ Saying, We give thee thanks, O LORD God Almighty, which art, and wast, and art to come; because

thou hast taken to thee thy great power, and hast reigned.

¹⁸ And the nations were angry, and thy wrath is come, and the time of the dead, that they should be judged, and that thou shouldest give reward unto thy servants the prophets, and to the saints, and them that fear thy name, small and great; and shouldest destroy them which destroy the earth.

¹⁹ And the temple of God was opened in heaven, and there was seen in his temple the ark of his testament: and there were lightnings, and voices, and thunderings, and an earthquake, and great hail.

12 And there appeared a great wonder in heaven; a woman clothed with the sun, and the moon under her feet, and upon her head a crown of twelve stars:

² And she being with child cried, travailing in birth, and pained to be delivered.

³ And there appeared another wonder in heaven; and behold a great red dragon, having seven heads and ten horns, and seven crowns upon his heads.

⁴ And his tail drew the third part of the stars of heaven, and did cast them to the earth: and the dragon stood before the woman which was ready to be delivered, for to devour her child as soon as it was born.

⁵ And she brought forth a man child, who was to rule all nations with a rod of iron: and her child was caught up unto God, and to his throne.

⁶ And the woman fled into the wilderness, where she hath a place prepared of God, that they should feed her there a thousand two hundred and threescore days.

⁷ And there was war in heaven: Michael and his angels fought against the dragon; and the dragon fought and his angels,

⁸ And prevailed not; neither was their place found any more in heaven.

⁹ And the great dragon was cast out, that old serpent, called the Devil, and Satan, which deceiveth the whole world: he was cast out into the earth, and his angels were cast out with him.

¹⁰ And I heard a loud voice saying in heaven, Now is come salvation, and strength, and the kingdom of our God, and the power of his Christ: for the accuser of our brethren is cast down, which accused them before our God day and night.

¹¹ And they overcame him by the blood of the Lamb, and by the word of their testimony; and they loved not their lives unto the death.

¹² Therefore rejoice, ye heavens, and ye that dwell in them. Woe to the inhabiters of the earth and of the sea! for the devil is come down unto you, having great wrath, because he knoweth that he hath but a short

time.

¹³ And when the dragon saw that he was cast unto the earth, he persecuted the woman which brought forth the man child.

¹⁴ And to the woman were given two wings of a great eagle, that she might fly into the wilderness, into her place, where she is nourished for a time, and times, and half a time, from the face of the serpent.

¹⁵ And the serpent cast out of his mouth water as a flood after the woman, that he might cause her to be carried away of the flood.

¹⁶ And the earth helped the woman, and the earth opened her mouth, and swallowed up the flood which the dragon cast out of his mouth.

¹⁷ And the dragon was wroth with the woman, and went to make war with the remnant of her seed, which keep the commandments of God, and have the testimony of Jesus Christ.

13 And I stood upon the sand of the sea, and saw a beast rise up out of the sea, having seven heads and ten horns, and upon his horns ten crowns, and upon his heads the name of blasphemy.

² And the beast which I saw was like unto a leopard, and his feet were as the feet of a bear, and his mouth as the mouth of a lion: and the dragon gave him his power, and his seat, and great authority.

³ And I saw one of his heads as it were wounded to death; and his deadly wound was healed: and all the world wondered after the beast.

⁴ And they worshipped the dragon which gave power unto the beast: and they worshipped the beast, saying, Who is like unto the beast? who is able to make war with him?

⁵ And there was given unto him a mouth speaking great things and blasphemies; and power was given unto him to continue forty and two months.

⁶ And he opened his mouth in blasphemy against God, to blaspheme his name, and his tabernacle, and them that dwell in heaven.

⁷ And it was given unto him to make war with the saints, and to overcome them: and power was given him over all kindreds, and tongues, and nations.

⁸ And all that dwell upon the earth shall worship him, whose names are not written in the book of life of the Lamb slain from the foundation of the world.

⁹ If any man have an ear, let him hear.

¹⁰ He that leadeth into captivity shall go into captivity: he that killeth with the sword must be killed

with the sword. Here is the patience and the faith of the saints.

[11] And I beheld another beast coming up out of the earth; and he had two horns like a lamb, and he spake as a dragon.

[12] And he exerciseth all the power of the first beast before him, and causeth the earth and them which dwell therein to worship the first beast, whose deadly wound was healed.

[13] And he doeth great wonders, so that he maketh fire come down from heaven on the earth in the sight of men,

[14] And deceiveth them that dwell on the earth by the means of those miracles which he had power to do in the sight of the beast; saying to them that dwell on the earth, that they should make an image to the beast, which had the wound by a sword, and did live.

[15] And he had power to give life unto the image of the beast, that the image of the beast should both speak, and cause that as many as would not worship the image of the beast should be killed.

[16] And he causeth all, both small and great, rich and poor, free and bond, to receive a mark in their right hand, or in their foreheads:

[17] And that no man might buy or sell, save he that had the mark, or the name of the beast, or the number of his name.

[18] Here is wisdom. Let him that hath understanding count the number of the beast: for it is the number of a man; and his number is Six hundred threescore and six.

14 And I looked, and, lo, a Lamb stood on the mount Sion, and with him an hundred forty and four thousand, having his Father's name written in their foreheads.

[2] And I heard a voice from heaven, as the voice of many waters, and as the voice of a great thunder: and I heard the voice of harpers harping with their harps:

[3] And they sung as it were a new song before the throne, and before the four beasts, and the elders: and no man could learn that song but the hundred and forty and four thousand, which were redeemed from the earth.

[4] These are they which were not defiled with women; for they are virgins. These are they which follow the Lamb whithersoever he goeth. These were redeemed from among men, being the firstfruits unto God and to the Lamb.

[5] And in their mouth was found no guile: for they are without fault before the throne of God.

⁶ And I saw another angel fly in the midst of heaven, having the everlasting gospel to preach unto them that dwell on the earth, and to every nation, and kindred, and tongue, and people,

⁷ Saying with a loud voice, Fear God, and give glory to him; for the hour of his judgment is come: and worship him that made heaven, and earth, and the sea, and the fountains of waters.

⁸ And there followed another angel, saying, Babylon is fallen, is fallen, that great city, because she made all nations drink of the wine of the wrath of her fornication.

⁹ And the third angel followed them, saying with a loud voice, If any man worship the beast and his image, and receive his mark in his forehead, or in his hand,

¹⁰ The same shall drink of the wine of the wrath of God, which is poured out without mixture into the cup of his indignation; and he shall be tormented with fire and brimstone in the presence of the holy angels, and in the presence of the Lamb:

¹¹ And the smoke of their torment ascendeth up for ever and ever: and they have no rest day nor night, who worship the beast and his image, and whosoever receiveth the mark of his name.

¹² Here is the patience of the saints: here are they that keep the commandments of God, and the faith of Jesus.

¹³ And I heard a voice from heaven saying unto me, Write, Blessed are the dead which die in the Lord from henceforth: Yea, saith the Spirit, that they may rest from their labours; and their works do follow them.

¹⁴ And I looked, and behold a white cloud, and upon the cloud one sat like unto the Son of man, having on his head a golden crown, and in his hand a sharp sickle.

¹⁵ And another angel came out of the temple, crying with a loud voice to him that sat on the cloud, Thrust in thy sickle, and reap: for the time is come for thee to reap; for the harvest of the earth is ripe.

¹⁶ And he that sat on the cloud thrust in his sickle on the earth; and the earth was reaped.

¹⁷ And another angel came out of the temple which is in heaven, he also having a sharp sickle.

¹⁸ And another angel came out from the altar, which had power over fire; and cried with a loud cry to him that had the sharp sickle, saying, Thrust in thy sharp sickle, and gather the clusters of the vine of the earth; for her grapes are fully ripe.

¹⁹ And the angel thrust in his sickle into the earth, and gathered the vine of the earth, and cast it into the great winepress of the wrath of God.

²⁰ And the winepress was trodden without the city, and blood came out of the winepress, even unto the horse bridles, by the space of a thousand and six hundred furlongs.

15 And I saw another sign in heaven, great and marvellous, seven angels having the seven last plagues; for in them is filled up the wrath of God.

² And I saw as it were a sea of glass mingled with fire: and them that had gotten the victory over the beast, and over his image, and over his mark, and over the number of his name, stand on the sea of glass, having the harps of God.

³ And they sing the song of Moses the servant of God, and the song of the Lamb, saying, Great and marvellous are thy works, Lord God Almighty; just and true are thy ways, thou King of saints.

⁴ Who shall not fear thee, O Lord, and glorify thy name? for thou only art holy: for all nations shall come and worship before thee; for thy judgments are made manifest.

⁵ And after that I looked, and, behold, the temple of the tabernacle of the testimony in heaven was opened:

⁶ And the seven angels came out of the temple, having the seven plagues, clothed in pure and white linen, and having their breasts girded with golden girdles.

⁷ And one of the four beasts gave unto the seven angels seven golden vials full of the wrath of God, who liveth for ever and ever.

⁸ And the temple was filled with smoke from the glory of God, and from his power; and no man was able to enter into the temple, till the seven plagues of the seven angels were fulfilled.

16 And I heard a great voice out of the temple saying to the seven angels, Go your ways, and pour out the vials of the wrath of God upon the earth.

² And the first went, and poured out his vial upon the earth; and there fell a noisome and grievous sore upon the men which had the mark of the beast, and upon them which worshipped his image.

³ And the second angel poured out his vial upon the sea; and it became as the blood of a dead man: and every living soul died in the sea.

⁴ And the third angel poured out his vial upon the rivers and fountains of waters; and they became blood.

⁵ And I heard the angel of the waters say, Thou art righteous, O Lord, which art, and wast, and shalt be, because thou hast judged thus.

⁶ For they have shed the blood of saints and prophets, and thou hast given them blood to drink; for

they are worthy.

⁷ And I heard another out of the altar say, Even so, Lord God Almighty, true and righteous are thy judgments.

⁸ And the fourth angel poured out his vial upon the sun; and power was given unto him to scorch men with fire.

⁹ And men were scorched with great heat, and blasphemed the name of God, which hath power over these plagues: and they repented not to give him glory.

¹⁰ And the fifth angel poured out his vial upon the seat of the beast; and his kingdom was full of darkness; and they gnawed their tongues for pain,

¹¹ And blasphemed the God of heaven because of their pains and their sores, and repented not of their deeds.

¹² And the sixth angel poured out his vial upon the great river Euphrates; and the water thereof was dried up, that the way of the kings of the east might be prepared.

¹³ And I saw three unclean spirits like frogs come out of the mouth of the dragon, and out of the mouth of the beast, and out of the mouth of the false prophet.

¹⁴ For they are the spirits of devils, working miracles, which go forth unto the kings of the earth and of the whole world, to gather them to the battle of that great day of God Almighty.

¹⁵ Behold, I come as a thief. Blessed is he that watcheth, and keepeth his garments, lest he walk naked, and they see his shame.

¹⁶ And he gathered them together into a place called in the Hebrew tongue Armageddon.

¹⁷ And the seventh angel poured out his vial into the air; and there came a great voice out of the temple of heaven, from the throne, saying, It is done.

¹⁸ And there were voices, and thunders, and lightnings; and there was a great earthquake, such as was not since men were upon the earth, so mighty an earthquake, and so great.

¹⁹ And the great city was divided into three parts, and the cities of the nations fell: and great Babylon came in remembrance before God, to give unto her the cup of the wine of the fierceness of his wrath.

²⁰ And every island fled away, and the mountains were not found.

²¹ And there fell upon men a great hail out of heaven, every stone about the weight of a talent: and men blasphemed God because of the plague of the hail; for the plague thereof was exceeding great.

17 And there came one of the seven angels which had the seven vials, and talked with me, saying unto me, Come hither; I will shew unto thee the judgment of the great whore that sitteth upon many waters:

² With whom the kings of the earth have committed fornication, and the inhabitants of the earth have been made drunk with the wine of her fornication.

³ So he carried me away in the spirit into the wilderness: and I saw a woman sit upon a scarlet coloured beast, full of names of blasphemy, having seven heads and ten horns.

⁴ And the woman was arrayed in purple and scarlet colour, and decked with gold and precious stones and pearls, having a golden cup in her hand full of abominations and filthiness of her fornication:

⁵ And upon her forehead was a name written, MYSTERY, BABYLON THE GREAT, THE MOTHER OF HARLOTS AND ABOMINATIONS OF THE EARTH.

⁶ And I saw the woman drunken with the blood of the saints, and with the blood of the martyrs of Jesus: and when I saw her, I wondered with great admiration.

⁷ And the angel said unto me, Wherefore didst thou marvel? I will tell thee the mystery of the woman, and of the beast that carrieth her, which hath the seven heads and ten horns.

⁸ The beast that thou sawest was, and is not; and shall ascend out of the bottomless pit, and go into perdition: and they that dwell on the earth shall wonder, whose names were not written in the book of life from the foundation of the world, when they behold the beast that was, and is not, and yet is.

⁹ And here is the mind which hath wisdom. The seven heads are seven mountains, on which the woman sitteth.

¹⁰ And there are seven kings: five are fallen, and one is, and the other is not yet come; and when he cometh, he must continue a short space.

¹¹ And the beast that was, and is not, even he is the eighth, and is of the seven, and goeth into perdition.

¹² And the ten horns which thou sawest are ten kings, which have received no kingdom as yet; but receive power as kings one hour with the beast.

¹³ These have one mind, and shall give their power and strength unto the beast.

¹⁴ These shall make war with the Lamb, and the Lamb shall overcome them: for he is Lord of lords, and King of kings: and they that are with him are called, and chosen, and faithful.

¹⁵ And he saith unto me, The waters which thou sawest, where the whore sitteth, are peoples, and mul-

titudes, and nations, and tongues.

¹⁶ And the ten horns which thou sawest upon the beast, these shall hate the whore, and shall make her desolate and naked, and shall eat her flesh, and burn her with fire.

¹⁷ For God hath put in their hearts to fulfil his will, and to agree, and give their kingdom unto the beast, until the words of God shall be fulfilled.

¹⁸ And the woman which thou sawest is that great city, which reigneth over the kings of the earth.

18 And after these things I saw another angel come down from heaven, having great power; and the earth was lightened with his glory.

² And he cried mightily with a strong voice, saying, Babylon the great is fallen, is fallen, and is become the habitation of devils, and the hold of every foul spirit, and a cage of every unclean and hateful bird.

³ For all nations have drunk of the wine of the wrath of her fornication, and the kings of the earth have committed fornication with her, and the merchants of the earth are waxed rich through the abundance of her delicacies.

⁴ And I heard another voice from heaven, saying, Come out of her, my people, that ye be not partakers of her sins, and that ye receive not of her plagues.

⁵ For her sins have reached unto heaven, and God hath remembered her iniquities.

⁶ Reward her even as she rewarded you, and double unto her double according to her works: in the cup which she hath filled fill to her double.

⁷ How much she hath glorified herself, and lived deliciously, so much torment and sorrow give her: for she saith in her heart, I sit a queen, and am no widow, and shall see no sorrow.

⁸ Therefore shall her plagues come in one day, death, and mourning, and famine; and she shall be utterly burned with fire: for strong is the Lord God who judgeth her.

⁹ And the kings of the earth, who have committed fornication and lived deliciously with her, shall bewail her, and lament for her, when they shall see the smoke of her burning,

¹⁰ Standing afar off for the fear of her torment, saying, Alas, alas that great city Babylon, that mighty city! for in one hour is thy judgment come.

¹¹ And the merchants of the earth shall weep and mourn over her; for no man buyeth their merchandise any more:

¹² The merchandise of gold, and silver, and precious stones, and of pearls, and fine linen, and purple,

and silk, and scarlet, and all thyine wood, and all manner vessels of ivory, and all manner vessels of most precious wood, and of brass, and iron, and marble,

¹³ And cinnamon, and odours, and ointments, and frankincense, and wine, and oil, and fine flour, and wheat, and beasts, and sheep, and horses, and chariots, and slaves, and souls of men.

¹⁴ And the fruits that thy soul lusted after are departed from thee, and all things which were dainty and goodly are departed from thee, and thou shalt find them no more at all.

¹⁵ The merchants of these things, which were made rich by her, shall stand afar off for the fear of her torment, weeping and wailing,

¹⁶ And saying, Alas, alas that great city, that was clothed in fine linen, and purple, and scarlet, and decked with gold, and precious stones, and pearls!

¹⁷ For in one hour so great riches is come to nought. And every shipmaster, and all the company in ships, and sailors, and as many as trade by sea, stood afar off,

¹⁸ And cried when they saw the smoke of her burning, saying, What city is like unto this great city!

¹⁹ And they cast dust on their heads, and cried, weeping and wailing, saying, Alas, alas that great city, wherein were made rich all that had ships in the sea by reason of her costliness! for in one hour is she made desolate.

²⁰ Rejoice over her, thou heaven, and ye holy apostles and prophets; for God hath avenged you on her.

²¹ And a mighty angel took up a stone like a great millstone, and cast it into the sea, saying, Thus with violence shall that great city Babylon be thrown down, and shall be found no more at all.

²² And the voice of harpers, and musicians, and of pipers, and trumpeters, shall be heard no more at all in thee; and no craftsman, of whatsoever craft he be, shall be found any more in thee; and the sound of a millstone shall be heard no more at all in thee;

²³ And the light of a candle shall shine no more at all in thee; and the voice of the bridegroom and of the bride shall be heard no more at all in thee: for thy merchants were the great men of the earth; for by thy sorceries were all nations deceived.

²⁴ And in her was found the blood of prophets, and of saints, and of all that were slain upon the earth.

19 And after these things I heard a great voice of much people in heaven, saying, Alleluia; Salvation, and glory, and honour, and power, unto the Lord our God:

² For true and righteous are his judgments: for he hath judged the great whore, which did corrupt the

earth with her fornication, and hath avenged the blood of his servants at her hand.

³ And again they said, Alleluia And her smoke rose up for ever and ever.

⁴ And the four and twenty elders and the four beasts fell down and worshippcd God that sat on the throne, saying, Amen; Alleluia.

⁵ And a voice came out of the throne, saying, Praise our God, all ye his servants, and ye that fear him, both small and great.

⁶ And I heard as it were the voice of a great multitude, and as the voice of many waters, and as the voice of mighty thunderings, saying, Alleluia: for the Lord God omnipotent reigneth.

⁷ Let us be glad and rejoice, and give honour to him: for the marriage of the Lamb is come, and his wife hath made herself ready.

⁸ And to her was granted that she should be arrayed in fine linen, clean and white: for the fine linen is the righteousness of saints.

⁹ And he saith unto me, Write, Blessed are they which are called unto the marriage supper of the Lamb. And he saith unto me, These are the true sayings of God.

¹⁰ And I fell at his feet to worship him. And he said unto me, See thou do it not: I am thy fellowservant, and of thy brethren that have the testimony of Jesus: worship God: for the testimony of Jesus is the spirit of prophecy.

¹¹ And I saw heaven opened, and behold a white horse; and he that sat upon him was called Faithful and True, and in righteousness he doth judge and make war.

¹² His eyes were as a flame of fire, and on his head were many crowns; and he had a name written, that no man knew, but he himself.

¹³ And he was clothed with a vesture dipped in blood: and his name is called The Word of God.

¹⁴ And the armies which were in heaven followed him upon white horses, clothed in fine linen, white and clean.

¹⁵ And out of his mouth goeth a sharp sword, that with it he should smite the nations: and he shall rule them with a rod of iron: and he treadeth the winepress of the fierceness and wrath of Almighty God.

¹⁶ And he hath on his vesture and on his thigh a name written, KING OF KINGS, AND LORD OF LORDS.

¹⁷ And I saw an angel standing in the sun; and he cried with a loud voice, saying to all the fowls that fly in the midst of heaven, Come and gather yourselves together unto the supper of the great God;

¹⁸ That ye may eat the flesh of kings, and the flesh of captains, and the flesh of mighty men, and the

flesh of horses, and of them that sit on them, and the flesh of all men, both free and bond, both small and great.

¹⁹ And I saw the beast, and the kings of the earth, and their armies, gathered together to make war against him that sat on the horse, and against his army.

²⁰ And the beast was taken, and with him the false prophet that wrought miracles before him, with which he deceived them that had received the mark of the beast, and them that worshipped his image. These both were cast alive into a lake of fire burning with brimstone.

²¹ And the remnant were slain with the sword of him that sat upon the horse, which sword proceeded out of his mouth: and all the fowls were filled with their flesh.

20 And I saw an angel come down from heaven, having the key of the bottomless pit and a great chain in his hand.

² And he laid hold on the dragon, that old serpent, which is the Devil, and Satan, and bound him a thousand years,

³ And cast him into the bottomless pit, and shut him up, and set a seal upon him, that he should deceive the nations no more, till the thousand years should be fulfilled: and after that he must be loosed a little season.

⁴ And I saw thrones, and they sat upon them, and judgment was given unto them: and I saw the souls of them that were beheaded for the witness of Jesus, and for the word of God, and which had not worshipped the beast, neither his image, neither had received his mark upon their foreheads, or in their hands; and they lived and reigned with Christ a thousand years.

⁵ But the rest of the dead lived not again until the thousand years were finished. This is the first resurrection.

⁶ Blessed and holy is he that hath part in the first resurrection: on such the second death hath no power, but they shall be priests of God and of Christ, and shall reign with him a thousand years.

⁷ And when the thousand years are expired, Satan shall be loosed out of his prison,

⁸ And shall go out to deceive the nations which are in the four quarters of the earth, Gog, and Magog, to gather them together to battle: the number of whom is as the sand of the sea.

⁹ And they went up on the breadth of the earth, and compassed the camp of the saints about, and the beloved city: and fire came down from God out of heaven, and devoured them.

¹⁰ And the devil that deceived them was cast into the lake of fire and brimstone, where the beast and the false prophet are, and shall be tormented day and night for ever and ever.

¹¹ And I saw a great white throne, and him that sat on it, from whose face the earth and the heaven fled away; and there was found no place for them.

¹² And I saw the dead, small and great, stand before God; and the books were opened: and another book was opened, which is the book of life: and the dead were judged out of those things which were written in the books, according to their works.

¹³ And the sea gave up the dead which were in it; and death and hell delivered up the dead which were in them: and they were judged every man according to their works.

¹⁴ And death and hell were cast into the lake of fire. This is the second death.

¹⁵ And whosoever was not found written in the book of life was cast into the lake of fire.

21 And I saw a new heaven and a new earth: for the first heaven and the first earth were passed away; and there was no more sea.

² And I John saw the holy city, new Jerusalem, coming down from God out of heaven, prepared as a bride adorned for her husband.

³ And I heard a great voice out of heaven saying, Behold, the tabernacle of God is with men, and he will dwell with them, and they shall be his people, and God himself shall be with them, and be their God.

⁴ And God shall wipe away all tears from their eyes; and there shall be no more death, neither sorrow, nor crying, neither shall there be any more pain: for the former things are passed away.

⁵ And he that sat upon the throne said, Behold, I make all things new. And he said unto me, Write: for these words are true and faithful.

⁶ And he said unto me, It is done. I am Alpha and Omega, the beginning and the end. I will give unto him that is athirst of the fountain of the water of life freely.

⁷ He that overcometh shall inherit all things; and I will be his God, and he shall be my son.

⁸ But the fearful, and unbelieving, and the abominable, and murderers, and whoremongers, and sorcerers, and idolaters, and all liars, shall have their part in the lake which burneth with fire and brimstone: which is the second death.

⁹ And there came unto me one of the seven angels which had the seven vials full of the seven last plagues, and talked with me, saying, Come hither, I will shew thee the bride, the Lamb's wife.

¹⁰ And he carried me away in the spirit to a great and high mountain, and shewed me that great city, the holy Jerusalem, descending out of heaven from God,

¹¹ Having the glory of God: and her light was like unto a stone most precious, even like a jasper stone, clear as crystal;

¹² And had a wall great and high, and had twelve gates, and at the gates twelve angels, and names written thereon, which are the names of the twelve tribes of the children of Israel:

¹³ On the east three gates; on the north three gates; on the south three gates; and on the west three gates.

¹⁴ And the wall of the city had twelve foundations, and in them the names of the twelve apostles of the Lamb.

¹⁵ And he that talked with me had a golden reed to measure the city, and the gates thereof, and the wall thereof.

¹⁶ And the city lieth foursquare, and the length is as large as the breadth: and he measured the city with the reed, twelve thousand furlongs. The length and the breadth and the height of it are equal.

¹⁷ And he measured the wall thereof, an hundred and forty and four cubits, according to the measure of a man, that is, of the angel.

¹⁸ And the building of the wall of it was of jasper: and the city was pure gold, like unto clear glass.

¹⁹ And the foundations of the wall of the city were garnished with all manner of precious stones. The first foundation was jasper; the second, sapphire; the third, a chalcedony; the fourth, an emerald;

²⁰ The fifth, sardonyx; the sixth, sardius; the seventh, chrysolyte; the eighth, beryl; the ninth, a topaz; the tenth, a chrysoprasus; the eleventh, a jacinth; the twelfth, an amethyst.

²¹ And the twelve gates were twelve pearls: every several gate was of one pearl: and the street of the city was pure gold, as it were transparent glass.

²² And I saw no temple therein: for the Lord God Almighty and the Lamb are the temple of it.

²³ And the city had no need of the sun, neither of the moon, to shine in it: for the glory of God did lighten it, and the Lamb is the light thereof.

²⁴ And the nations of them which are saved shall walk in the light of it: and the kings of the earth do bring their glory and honour into it.

²⁵ And the gates of it shall not be shut at all by day: for there shall be no night there.

²⁶ And they shall bring the glory and honour of the nations into it.

²⁷ And there shall in no wise enter into it any thing that defileth, neither whatsoever worketh abomina-

tion, or maketh a lie: but they which are written in the Lamb's book of life.

22 And he shewed me a pure river of water of life, clear as crystal, proceeding out of the throne of God and of the Lamb.

2 In the midst of the street of it, and on either side of the river, was there the tree of life, which bare twelve manner of fruits, and yielded her fruit every month: and the leaves of the tree were for the healing of the nations.

3 And there shall be no more curse: but the throne of God and of the Lamb shall be in it; and his servants shall serve him:

4 And they shall see his face; and his name shall be in their foreheads.

5 And there shall be no night there; and they need no candle, neither light of the sun; for the Lord God giveth them light: and they shall reign for ever and ever.

6 And he said unto me, These sayings are faithful and true: and the Lord God of the holy prophets sent his angel to shew unto his servants the things which must shortly be done.

7 Behold, I come quickly: blessed is he that keepeth the sayings of the prophecy of this book.

8 And I John saw these things, and heard them. And when I had heard and seen, I fell down to worship before the feet of the angel which shewed me these things.

9 Then saith he unto me, See thou do it not: for I am thy fellowservant, and of thy brethren the prophets, and of them which keep the sayings of this book: worship God.

10 And he saith unto me, Seal not the sayings of the prophecy of this book: for the time is at hand.

11 He that is unjust, let him be unjust still: and he which is filthy, let him be filthy still: and he that is righteous, let him be righteous still: and he that is holy, let him be holy still.

12 And, behold, I come quickly; and my reward is with me, to give every man according as his work shall be.

13 I am Alpha and Omega, the beginning and the end, the first and the last.

14 Blessed are they that do his commandments, that they may have right to the tree of life, and may enter in through the gates into the city.

15 For without are dogs, and sorcerers, and whoremongers, and murderers, and idolaters, and whosoever loveth and maketh a lie.

16 I Jesus have sent mine angel to testify unto you these things in the churches. I am the root and the

offspring of David, and the bright and morning star.

¹⁷ And the Spirit and the bride say, Come. And let him that heareth say, Come. And let him that is athirst come. And whosoever will, let him take the water of life freely.

¹⁸ For I testify unto every man that heareth the words of the prophecy of this book, If any man shall add unto these things, God shall add unto him the plagues that are written in this book:

¹⁹ And if any man shall take away from the words of the book of this prophecy, God shall take away his part out of the book of life, and out of the holy city, and from the things which are written in this book.

²⁰ He which testifieth these things saith, Surely I come quickly. Amen. Even so, come, Lord Jesus.

²¹ The grace of our Lord Jesus Christ be with you all. Amen.

ARE YOU WILLING TO COME TO THE LIVING WATER?

"'Oh, EVERY one that thirsts, come to the waters. He that has no money; come, buy and eat. Yes, come, buy wine and milk without money and without price. Incline your ear, and come to me. Hear, and your soul shall live; and I will make an everlasting covenant with you, even the sure mercies of David. Seek the LORD while he may be found, call upon him while he is near. Let the wicked forsake his way, and the unrighteous man his thoughts. And let him return to the LORD, and he will have mercy upon him; and to our God, for he will abundantly pardon. 'For my thoughts are not your thoughts, neither are your ways my ways,' says the LORD. 'For as the heavens are higher than the earth, so are my ways higher than your ways, and my thoughts than your thoughts. For as the rain comes down, and the snow from heaven, and does not return, but waters the earth, and makes it bring forth and bud, that it might give seed to the sower, and bread to the eater; So shall my word be that goes forth out of my mouth. It shall not return to me void, but it shall accomplish that which I please, and it shall prosper in the thing to where I send it,'" (Isaiah 55:1,3, 6–11).

Psalm 146:5–10 "Happy is he that has the God of Jacob for his help, whose hope is in the LORD his God: which made heaven, and earth, the sea, and all that is therein. Which keeps TRUTH forever, which executes judgment for the oppressed, which gives food to the hungry. The LORD looses the prisoners. The LORD opens the eyes of the blind. The LORD raises those who are bowed down. The LORD loves the righteous. The LORD preserves the strangers. He relieves the fatherless and widow, but the way of the wicked he turns upside down. The LORD shall reign for ever. Even your God, Oh Zion, unto all generations. Praise the LORD."

©2018 Eternal Living Water-Eternal Perspective: Connecting the Crimson Dots of His Covenant

PARTING THOUGHTS

From the beginning, God has been in the presence of His creation. After Adam and Eve made the decision to partake in eating of the tree of the knowledge of good and evil, God's presence on the earth was manifested is several different ways. Throughout history, many references are recorded in the scriptures as "the glory of the LORD." They are too numerous to list here, but look up the word glory (Strong's #3519) and follow the trail to see what it says.

A small sample of references are included. The first one takes us back to the book of Exodus. We read about the tabernacle, the ark of the testimony (covenant), and the mercy seat that covered the top of the ark, which displayed the presence and glory of the LORD. His glory was also described in Exodus 24:17 which says, "And the sight of the glory of the LORD was like devouring fire on the top of the mount in the eyes of the children of Israel." In Deuteronomy 4:35–36 it says, "Unto you it was shown, that you might know that the LORD, he is God. There is none else beside him. Out of heaven he made you to hear his voice, that he might instruct you. And upon earth, he showed you his great fire; and you heard his words out of the midst of the fire." In Hebrews 12:22–24 it is recorded, "But you are to come to mount Zion, and to the city of the living God, the heavenly Jerusalem, and to an innumerable company of angels, to the general assembly and church of the firstborn, which are written in heaven, and to God the Judge of all, and to the spirits of just men made perfect, and to Jesus (Yeshua) the mediator of the new covenant, and to the blood of sprinkling, that speaks of better things than that of Abel." The final example referenced here is recorded in Revelation 21:3–23, "And I heard a great voice out of heaven saying, 'Behold, the tabernacle of God is with men, and he will dwell with them, and they shall be his people, and God himself shall be with them, and be their God... And I saw no temple therein: for the Lord God Almighty and the Lamb are the temple of it. And the city had no need of the sun, neither of the moon, to shine in it. For the glory of God did lighten it, and the Lamb is the light thereof."

THE DECISION IS YOURS. WHAT WILL YOU CHOOSE? It is a matter of LIFE and death.